Alexander J. Reid

Illustrated Annual Review of the Appleton Post

Alexander J. Reid

Illustrated Annual Review of the Appleton Post

ISBN/EAN: 9783337372385

Printed in Europe, USA, Canada, Australia, Japan

Cover: Foto ©ninafisch / pixelio.de

More available books at **www.hansebooks.com**

ILLUSTRATED ANNUAL REVIEW

OF THE

APPLETON POST,

DEVOTED TO THE

CITY OF APPLETON,

WISCONSIN,

Its Water Power and Industries;

ALSO

An Historical Sketch of Fox River Valley.

PREPARED AND ARRANGED

BY A. J. REID.

———

APPLETON, WIS:
POST PUBLISHING CO., STEAM PRINTERS.
1879.

TABLE OF CONTENTS.

ILLUSTRATIONS.

EARLY TIMES IN FOX RIVER VALLEY.

History is among the most pleasing and entertaining of human studies. By it we become familiar with men and things, in ages long past, and live, as it were, from the beginning of time to the present hour. It embraces the biography of men and nations—their ups and downs—their rise and fall, detailing the incidents and events which have been, the changes which have occurred and the improvements which have taken place. And while those who are accustomed to study history are familiar with the past in foreign lands, but comparatively few are well informed on the early events and history of the locality in which they reside. Ancient history is chiefly made up of wars and sieges, battles and fights between nations and individuals, but modern history is, in great part, composed of the peaceful events of human progress— the onward march of discovery, intelligence, commerce, the arts and sciences as applied to the general well being of the human family.

THE ABORIGINES.

In other lands the ingenuity of man evolved from nature the means of putting their traditions and history in tangible form and transmitting them to posterity. In this land the untutored Savage not only failed to record the traditions and history of his race, but almost deemed it disrespect to talk of the dead. In the numerous *tumuli* and earthmarks, scattered all over the land, nothing has been discovered but human bones and arrow heads, indicating beyond doubt, the existence of a numerous and warlike people, and of that people the present race of Indians know nothing whatever. Even this latter race has almost entirely disappeared, and no record of them will remain except that which the white man preserves. They have withered and wilted before the march of civilization. They have drunk to the very dregs its vices, while they have shunned and resented its virtues. They are now a degraded and wretched people, a burden to themselves and the nation. Not so were they at the first coming of the white man. Then they were the brave warrior, the keen hunter, swift of foot and strong of limb—the relentless enemy, the unflinching friend, the guileless and untutored children of the forest.

When the white man first visited Wisconsin, about the middle of the seventeenth century, the present limits of the State were principally occupied by two great tribes, the Menomonees and the Winnebagos. The former occupied and held all the territory on the east side of

Lake Winnebago and the Fox and Wolf Rivers, including Green Bay and the west shore of Lake Michigan; and the latter held all west of Lake Winnebago and the upper Fox and Wisconsin rivers. Both of these tribes were then powerful and for many years afterwards held in great awe the few white inhabitants who then inhabited the country. The Winnebagos, in 1824, numbered perhaps about six thousand, the Menomonees between three and four thousand. Their characters and habits differed very essentially. The Winnebagos were cruel and treacherous, and would rather despatch an enemy in secure ambush than face him in fair and euqal combat. The late Henry S. Baird, writing of this tribe as they were in 1824, says:

"They were friendly to the British and for many years were their pensioners, going openly every year to Canada to receive their presents from the British Government. They hated the Americans, and in the war of 1812, they espoused the cause of the former and proved the most sanguinary foes of the United States in the massacres of Mackinaw, Chicago and other places. Even in later years they viewed the citizens with suspicion and kept them in constant fear; and it is well known that they not only instigated the Sacs and Foxes in the Black Hawk war to commence hostilities but participated in their battles. But these were not the worst features in the character of this tribe. They united the art of stealing to that of lying. If they could catch the traveler's horse or lay hands upon any of his luggage or property, it was appropriated at once to their own use. Far different were the characters and habits of the Menomonees. As a tribe they practiced neither of the low vices of thieving or lying. Unlike their neighbors, whose character I have just portrayed, they were neither treacherous nor belligerent. Always friendly to the whites, they gained the friendship of the latter. It is true, that during the war of 1812, this tribe, together with all the northern and western tribes, joined the British, and fought under their standard; but this must be attributed to the fact that the whole of this portion of the northwest was, at that period, in subjec-

tion to that power. British fur traders then monopolized nearly the entire fur trade of this region, and British gold was lavishly expended by active and efficient agents, scattered over the whole country, to influence the Indian' tribes, and enlist them in the cause of their former invaders, the English. On the other hand, the Government of the United States had but a nominal possession of the country—but few forts, or places of defence, and these but feebly manned or defended, and the whole population left to their own resources. It was but natural that the Indians should take sides with the most powerful party, and with those who promised them that the Americans should be entirely expelled and driven from the country and the original inhabitants restored to their former homes. But this was not universally the case with the Menomonees, for although they generally united under the British flag, there were many exceptions. The descendents of some of the old American settlers well know that their families were not only rescued from the scalping knife, but subsequently protected by different individuals of the Menomonee tribe. In the Black Hawk war, they assembled *en masse*, and showed themselves efficient allies of the whites in bringing to a close what, at one time, threatened to be a renewal of those savage and sanguinary scenes, which at earlier periods devastated and laid waste many settlements of this North-west."

CUSTOMS.

From the late Judge Lockwood's observations of the habits and customs of the Indians, in about the years 1816 to 1820, we abstract the following:

MARRIAGES.

"When a young Indian desires to marry, he invites his relatives who are near or in camp, to a feast and informs them that he wishes a certain girl for his wife. If they are in favor of the match, they immediately collect goods and suitable articles for a present to the relatives of the desired one. One gives a gun, another a blanket, another a kettle or a horse, as he may happen to possess at the time. When the collection is completed some of the relatives carry the presents to the lodge of the father of the young woman. One of them expresses in song the object for which they are intended, and leaving the things at the door retires. If the father is favorably disposed to the match he invites all his relatives that are near, to a feast, and when assembled, if they conclude to give the girl in marriage, each takes of the articles, such as he can return in kind, and with such presents, together with the bride, they march to the lodge of the young man, where she is given up to him with many mintue ceremonies. After which, she returns again to her father's lodge, where they usually reside, the son-in-law hunting for the father-in-law until about the time the oldest child can walk, after which he generally gets a lodge for himself. A small apartment is petitioned off in the lodge of the father-in-law for the young couple. The young man generally during the day is out hunting and seldom visits the lodge of his bride until all the others have gone to sleep, when he crawls into the lodge. There is no familiarity between the parents of the bride and their son-in-law. If he is ever in their presence he appears ashamed and seldom speaks to them. If he wants to communicate to them it is done through his wife.

DEATHS AND BURIALS.

When a person dies, the body is decorated in all of his or their finery and four forks or crotches are cut and stuck in the ground upon which a scaffold is made, and the deceased wrapped in a newly painted buffalo skin, a new blanket is laid thereon with some ceremony. If the death takes place at a trader's house in the fall before they go to their hunt, an old woman, a relative of the deceased, is left there to feed and cry over the dead during the absence of the others. She usually goes about dark in the evening with a dish of provisions and sits down under the scaffold and commences crying and howling, with loud lamentatain, calling upon the Great Spirit to have mercy upon the deceased, etc. After continuing this doleful noise for about an hour, she leaves the dish of food under the scaffold and returns to the lodge and the dogs or wolves eat the provisions when the Indians suppose the dead ate them. The corpse is left in this manner until nothing remains but the bones when they are collected and carried to their village."

INDIAN VILLAGES.

The principal trading posts up to about the year 1830 were located at Mil-

waukee, Sheboygan, and Manitowoc on Lake Michigan; Menomonee River. Peshtigo and Oconto on Green Bay; Fond du Lac River, Lake Shawano and the portage of the Fox and Wisconsin. And one of the most populous villages was located on what is now known as Doty Island. This latter was ruled over for many years by a woman, but this was previous to the advent of the white man. She must have been a person of extraordinary parts and influence, for the tradition of the Indians endow her with great talents and powers. This was then a lovely spot, a favorite meeting place of all the Indian tribes. Here they assembled for their periodical councils and pow-wows, and the large elm tree on the opposite point was always designated by them as

"THE COUNCIL TREE".

Twenty years ago this tree was in the full maturity of its beauty and grandeur. Its form and outline were exceedingly graceful and beautiful, and its immense size and peaceful surroundings rendered it a great object of attraction. Then it was in a great part surrounded with a dense underbrush thickly matted with creepers and vines, forming a beautiful setting to the giant forest-king that towered over them. Beneath its branches a thousand men could find shelter from storm and refreshing shade from the summer sun. But now, alas how changed; the underbrush is all cut away, the march of modern improvement has encroached upon its very shadows, it looks lonely and forsaken, and like the children of the forest whom it so often sheltered, it seems "a stranger in its own land and a foreigner on its own soil."

LA BUTTE DES MORTS MASSACRE.

The points of land at the confluence of the Fox and Wolf rivers in Winnebago county is known as *butte des morts*, the French for hill of the dead. It gained its name from the following events which happened in the year 1725. For many years the Indians in possession of this point were in the habit of stopping and demanding tribute for liberty to pass. This had to be submitted to, but in the autumn of 1724, a hot headed young Canadian refused to pay the customary tribute and in the tussle he severely wounded the Indian who attempted to take it forcibly. He was thereupon instantly shot dead and scalped, and his boat was pillaged. When the news of this outrage reached Quebec, the SENER MORAN, a man of decided and energetic character, was dispatched with a considerable force to punish the perpetrators. In October, of the following year, he arrived in the Fox river and immediately sent a messenger to the hillock of the dead to demand the instant surrender of all persons concerned in the murder of the Canadian trader last year. This message the Indians treated with scorn. MORAN thereupon resolved to administer to them a chastisement they should never forget. He succeeded in enlisting in his expedition a large band of Menomonee Indians, the hereditary enemies of the Sacs, who were then in possession of the coveted point. These with a number of his soldiers he landed on a small creek about a mile below and ordered them to gain the woods in the rear of the village and there await until the firing commenced. When sufficient time had elapsed for his orders to be obeyed, the remaining troops crouched in the bottom of the boats with their arms ready, and hidden by the canvas used by the traders to cover their wares. This done he put off and the crew, disguised like boatmen, rowed up the river singing this ditty:

"*Tous les printemps*
Tant de nouvelles
Tous les amants
Changent de maitresses
Le bon vin m' endort
L'amour me revielle."

Tous les amants
Changent de maitresses
Ou ils changent qui voudront
Pour me garde le mienne
Le bon vin m' endort
L'amour me recielle.

This charming little love song has been admirably rendered into English by Mrs. Krum, of Madison, as follows:

"Each returning springtime
Brings so much that's new
All the fickle lovers.
Changing sweet hearts too;
The good wine soothes and gives me rest,
While love inspires and fills my breast."

"All the fickle lovers
Changing sweet-hearts still
I'll keep mine forever
Those may change who will.
The good wine soothes and gives me rest
While love inspires and fills my breast."

They were soon within sight of the villiage. The Indians little dreamt of the terrible fate that was soon to befall them. They were drunk or at least suffering from the effects of intoxication and when they saw the boats approaching, they cried out "Here come the traders with fire-water and blankets, let us make haste to the spoil." As the foremost boat came opposite, a dozen balls were fired athwart her course. M. MORAN rose and commanded the interpreter to ask what they wanted? *Skootay waubo Skootay waubo* (fire-warer) shouted five hundred voices. 'Shore' said MORAN and as the other boats were now along side they all touched the ground together. Then the Indians laid hands on them and commenced dragging them farther aground. Help! Help! thieves! thieves! cried Moran in full deep tones. At once the coverings were thrown off and a hundred and fifty soldiers were brought to sight, as if by the spell of an enchanter. 'Fire' cried Moran. The muskets flashed and twenty Sacs fell dead where they stood. To the poor misguided savages, the number of their enemies seemed trebled the reality. They fled picipitately to the villiage to prepare for defence. Two minutes sufficed for the troops to form and pursue.

The Sacs found at their lodges another and more terrible enemy than the French. A Menomonee had entered the place unsuspected and set it on fire on the windward side. The wind was high and in a few moments the frail bark dwellings were wrapped in a sheet of flame. The

Sacs then retreated towards the woods but there Moran's reserve met them and they were placed between two fires. Then burst forth one heartrending, agonizing shriek, and the devoted Sacs prepared to defend themselves with the courage of despair. Ball and bayonet now began their bloody work. The victims were hemmed in on every side. The Menomonees precluded the possibility of escape on the flanks; and the knife and glittering tomahawk cut off what the sword had spared. The inhabitants of the village fought with unshrinking courage. Few asked quarter and none received it. They perished man, woman and child. A heap of smoking ruins and a few houseless dogs, howling after the dead bodies of their masters, were the only objects the sad hillock presented.

But five families that had been absent at the time survived the slaughter. These gathered the remains of the dead, and piled a friendly mound of earth upon them, then left their country and emigrated towards the Mississippi, where they incorporated themselves with the Foxes.

THE FIRST SETTLERS.

Of the early French Canadian traders and settlers the late Henry S. Baird truly and appropriately remarks: "The character of the people was a compound of civilization and primitive simplicity—exhibiting the polite and lowly characteristics of the French and the thoughtlessness and improvidence of the Aborigines. Possessing the virtues of hospitality and the warmth of heart unknown to residents of cities, untrammeled by the etiquette and conventional rules of modern "high life," they were ever ready to receive and entertain their friends, and more intent upon the enjoyment of the present than to lay up a store, or make provision for the future. With few wants and contented and happy hearts, they found enjoyment in the merry dance, the sleigh ride, and the exciting horse race, and doubtless experienced more true happiness and contentment than the plodding, calculating and moneyed seeking people of the present day. This was the character of the settlers who occupied this country before the arrival of the Yankees—a class now entirely extinct or lost sight of by the present population, but it is one which unites the present with the past and for whom the "old settlers" entertain feelings of veneration and respect. They deserve to be remembered and placed on the pages of history as the first real pioneers of Wisconsin. Several of these persons have left descendants who still survive them, and the names of Lawe, Grignon, Juneau, Polier and others of that class will survive and serve as memorials of this old race of settlers long after the last of the present generation shall have been "gathered to their fathers."

JOSEPH ROLETTE.

The most noted of these old Canadian settlers was Joseph Rolette. He traded between Green Bay, the Upper Mississippi and Prairie du Chien. He was a Canadian by birth, of French extraction. He was educated for the Roman Catholic Church, but not liking the profession he quit it, and in 1804 came to Prairie du Chien. Although he was active in business and used every exertion to make money it was not with the miserly disposition of hoarding it for he was equally liberal in scattering it. He was hospitable and generous and liberal to the poor. He was the first to introduce swine and sheep into the country. He died at Prairie du Chien in 1841.

Mrs. Kinzie relates, in her *Wau Bun*, the following capital story of Mr. Rolette. The scene was on Lake Winnebago where Rolette was engaged with a trading boat, when he met another boat on which were his employees, directly from Prairie du Chien. Of course, after an absence of some weeks from home, the meeting on these lonely waters and the exchanging of news was an occasion of great excitement. The boats were stopped, earnest greetings interchanged, question followed question :

"*Eh bien*" enquired M. Rollette, "have they finished the new house ?"

"*Oui Monsieur.*"

" *Et la cheminee" fume-t-elle* ? (Does the chimney smoke.)

"*Non Monsieur.*"

" And the harvest, how is that ?"

" Very fine indeed."

" Is the Mill at work ?"

" Yes, plenty of water."

" How is whip ?" (His favorite horse.)

"Oh ! Whip is first rate."

Every thing in short about the store, the farm, the business of vairous descriptions being satisfactorily gone over, there was no occasion for farther delay. It was time to proceed.

"*Eh bien—adieu! bon voyage!*"

Arraches mes gens. (Go ahead now !) Then suddenly — *Arretz — arretz.* (Stop ! Stop !)

Comment portent Madame Rollette et les enfants? (How are Mrs. Rollette and the children ?

Mrs. Kinsie also gives another glimpse of M. Rollette's character. The Indians. she says, called him, Ah-kay-zaup-ee-tah, or Five More, because, as they said, let them offer what number of skins they might, in bartering for an article, his terms were invariably "five more."

Upon one occasion a lady remarked to him : Oh, M. Rolette I would not be engaged in the Indian trade, it seems to be a system of cheating the poor Indians. Let me tell you Madame, replied he with great *naivelle*, "it is not so easy a thing to cheat the Indians as you imagine, I have tried it these twenty years and have never succeeded."

EARLY LAWS AND CUSTOMS.

Up to about the year 1823, in the social and business relations the French laws, "*Coutume de Paris*," controlled the transaction of the settlers. And the few judicial officers then in the country, knew but little and cared less about legal codes, and jurisdictional limits The customs and habits of the people among which they lived were to them the supreme law of the land. They decided disputes, and settled differences. They solemnized marriages and granted divorces, and in the performance of this latter official duty they generally charged double the fee for granting a divorce that they would charge for marrying, wisely—concluding that when people wanted to get unmarried *they would willingly give double what they would in the first instance to form the matrimonial contract.*

The *Coutume de Paris* so far prevailed in this country generally, that a part of the ceremony of marriage was the entering into a contract in writing, generally giving, if no issue, the property to the survivor; and if they desired to be divorced they went together before the magistrate and made known their wishes, and be in their presence tore up the marriage contract. According to the custom of the country, they were then divorced. The late Judge Lockwood of Prairie du Chien, said he was once present at Judge Abbots—at Mack inlaw—when a couple presented themselves before him and were divorced in this manner. If an American Judge would thus act in this manner under American law, why should we be astonished at the vagaries of the noted Justice Reaume, when he donned his scarlet coat and cap and delivered judgment in the matter in litigation before him, *that the plaintiff should fetch him a load of hay, and the defendant should chop for him a cord of wood, and the Constable should pay the costs.* But *tempora mutantur,* the old *Regime* has passed away forever; and we merely recount these incidents ? or the pleasure and instruction of a subsequent generation.

INDIAN DEEDS.

In order to show in what manner and for what consideration Indian titles and claims to land were at times procured by the French traders, the following is a copy of a deed now on record in the office of the Register of Deeds of this county. It purports to convey to the grantee a large tract of land on both sides of the river at Kaukauna, then called Kakalin, and pronounced Kauka-lo.

"En mille sept cent quatre vingt triezc, trouvent present Wabispine et le Tabac noir, lesquels ont voluntairement aban-donez et cedez a Monsieur Domineque Ducharme, depuis le haut de portage de Kakalin jusque du bout de le Praire d'en bas, sur quarante arpens de profond-eur; et sur l'autre cote' vis a vis de lit portage quatre arpens de large, sur trente de profondeur. Lesquels vendeurs se sont trouves contens et satisfaits pour deux barrils de rum. Enfois de quois, ils ont faits leur marques, le vieux Wab-isipine etant avengle les Temvons ont fait sa marque pour lui.

MARK DE WABISIPINE.

DE L'ATRIBUTE
L'AIGLE.

MARQTE DE TABAC NOIR.

LAMBERT MACAULEY, } Temoins.
J. HARRISON,

TRANSLATION.

In one thousand, seven hundred and ninety-three are found present. Wabis-

ipine and the Black Tobacco who have voluntarily given up and ceded to Mr. Domenick Ducharme from the head of the Portage of Kakalin to the end of the Prairie below by forty arpens in depth; and on the other side opposite the said portage four arpens wide by thirty in depth. The said vendors are contented and satisfied for two barrels of rum. In faith of which they have made their marks, the old Wabisipine being blind the witnesses have made his mark for him.

MARK OF WABISIPINE,
of the attribute of the Eagle.
MARK OF THE BLACK TOBACCO.
Witness: J. HARRISON,
LAMBERT MACAULEY.
Congress in 1820, repudiated this deed and denied the claims.

FIRST AMERICAN SETTLERS

It was about the year 1824 that Americans commenced to come to Wisconsin. At that time there were but two settlements within the limits of the present state, namely Green Bay and Prairie-du Chien. There were no roads or public highways, save the navigable waters or the blind Indian trail. The trader had no choice in his mode of transit from place to place; no public means of conveyance from which he might select the most expeditious or agreeable. His only alternative was to travel on foot through the forest or pursue his voyage in the frail bark canoe. Then the United States mails were conveyed, during the season of navigation, by irregular and tardy conveyance of sail vessels and in winter they were carried on a man's back, through the trackless wilderness between Green Bay and Chicago, a distance of about two hundred miles, once a month.

Wisconsin was then a part of the Territory of Michigan. The laws then in force were crude and ill devised, some of which were really disgraceful to those who enacted them —such, for instance,

as *public whipping and selling the of-
fender into servitude for a period not
exceeding three months* simply for the
commission of mere petty offences.
These laws were enacted by a Legislative Board, consisting of the Governor
and Judges of the Territory who received their appointment from the general
government, and were in no way amen-
able to the people who were to be governed by their enactment. In the session
of 1822-23, Congress passed a law organ-
izing the then counties of Mackinaw,
Brown and Crawford, and made them a
separate judicial district, and the Hon.
James Duane Doty was appointed Judge.
The establishment of regularly organized courts may be considered a new era
in the history of the territory for it was
then for the first time that the citizen
regarded himself as really under the
protecting arm of the law, and in full
enjoyment of his liberty and property.
On the 4th day of October, 1824,
Judge Doty opened and organized the
first Court of general jurisdiction ever
held in Wisconsin. The difficulties he
had to overcome were almost insuper-
able. He had no court house, no officers.
There were only about half a dozen
American families at Green Bay, and all
the rest of the population were not only
unfriendly but viewed with jealousy and
suspicion the introduction of American
Courts and institutions, as a serious in-
terference with their peculiar customs
and relations. One of the greatest difficulties was to find a sufficient number
of English speaking citizens to summon
as jurors; after this difficulty was overcome. Court was formally opened in the
late Col. Irwin's log tavern, in a room
about twenty feet square. This house
was situated near the then village of
Shanty-town, but all traces of it have
disappeared many years since.

JAMES DUANE DOTY.

Judge Doty was then but twenty-five
years of age—tall and large of frame, a

splendid specimen of physical manhood.
To natural ease and dignity of deport-
ment, he added a pleasing address and
winning manners. His address to the
grand jury was informal and in a manner conversational. He impressed upon
them the necessity of preserving order
and peace, and good government, to the
end that every man, be he poor or rich,
strong or weak, should feel perfectly secure in his person and property; and
the only certain way of attaining this
object was to bring the violaters of law
to speedy trial and punishment. He further impressed upon them the necessity
of enforcing the statutes enacted for the
prevention of immorality and vice. He
charged them that if they knew or were
informed of persons living together as
husband and wife who had not been legal-
ly married, that they were guilty of a
crime under the law and should be
brought to trial; that the well being of
the community demanded it. This address created a deep impression, and
was the cause of immense excitement in
Green Bay, for a large portion of the
population had never been married but
lived with women whom they called
their wives. The grand jury, after due
deliberation, returned into court with
forty-four indictments: One for murder,
several for lesser offences, and *thirty-
eight for illicit cohabitation.* The in-
dignation of the old settlers knew no
bounds. They raved and swore and openly rebelled, but the close proximity of
Ft. Howard soon brought them to their
senses. Nearly all the offenders, in a
short time, adopted the intimation of
the judge, and got married, and thereby
escaped the penalty of the law. The
man indicted for murder was tried at
the next term of court, found guilty and
sentenced to be hanged. The then
Sheriff disliking the job, Ebenezer
Childs was appointed by the judge to
perform that duty, and the records show
that he did it "with neatness and dis-
patch."

:PUTAT

T IS $

. CEN

ng no inter
NOUGH
1at skill ar
an any ho
isiness on

t of Us

ETS,

NE

PLET

ET FOR S

nd & Bro.
Hyde & Harriman.
& Morrison.

Geo. Kreiss.

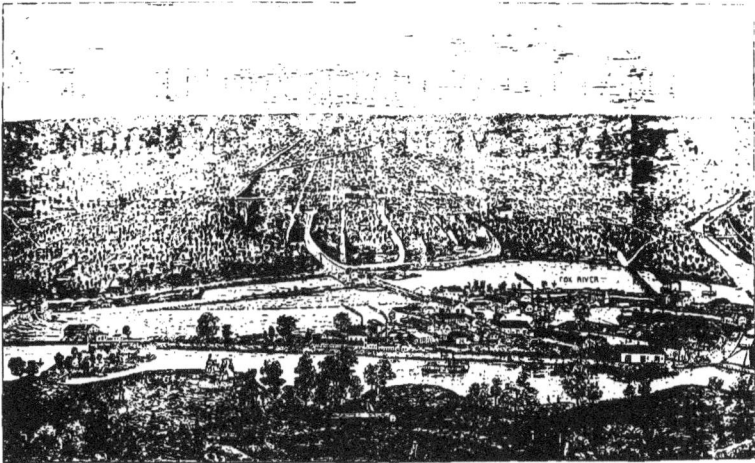

BIRD'S-EYE VIEW OF APPLETON, WISCONSIN.

1. Appleton Iron Company's Works.
2. Appleton Chair and Bedstead Factory.
3. Foundry and Machine Shop, Ketchaw & Morgan.
4. Appleton Hub and Spoke Factory, Marston & Beveridge.
5. Champion Steel Horse Nail Works.
6. Flour Barrel Stave Factory, G. W. Spaulding & Co.
7. Western Wood Pulp Mills, J. Brainer Smith & Co.
8. Appleton Paper and Pulp Co.'s Mills.

9. Geneseo Flouring Mills, Theodore Conkey.
10. Appleton Manufacturing Co.'s Works.
11. Atlas Paper Co.'s Mills.
12. Flouring Mills, S. R. Wilty.
13. Flouring Mills, Mauert & Weiland.
14. Flouring Mills, Cross & Wilty.
15. Sash, Door and Blind Factory, Briggs & Beveridge.
16. Pump Factory, T. W. Brown.

17. Furniture Factory.
18. Paper Mill, O. N. Richmond & Bro.
19. Telulah Mineral Springs, Ryde & Harriman.
20. Spoke Factory, Billings & Morrison.
21. Appleton Woolen Mills.
22. Tannery.
23. Hub and Spoke Factory, Geo. Kreiss.
24. Saw Mill, Rose & Heath.

☞Note- Since the above cut was engraved, several new establishments have been erected on the river which are mentioned elsewhere.

'ION WE SEEK.

;1,000 PER YEAR.

[T. ON $80,000.

est, which makes $5,000 per year.
I FOR US.
id energy will accomplish, con-
use in the State, save one
the same principle.

Being as Represented.

MILLINERY.

& CO.,

ON, WISCONSIN.

IYLE AND QUALITY.

From Green Bay, Judge Doty proceeded to Prairie du Chien, then called Fort Crawford. His young wife accompanied him. They made the whole journey in a birch bark canoe, paddled by four Canadian *voyageuers*. It took eight days to accomplish the journey. There was only one house (that of Mr. Grignon at Kaukauna) along the whole route of nearly three hundred miles. At night they would camp on the bank of the river, catch fish and shoot game, and cook and eat their meals and sleep with a zest and gratification that was a pleasant memory during all their lives. At Fort Crawford, the difficulties to be overcome were greater than those at Green Bay. The American settlers were fewer, and the opposition manifested by the other settlers to American manners and laws was more determined and annoying. Here Judge Doty calculated to make his home, as being the most central point in his Circuit. His first work was to procure a mail route to Ft. Crawford, and he, himself, was appointed and acted as postmaster. After a short time he concluded to return to Green Bay, and there the following year Ebenezer Childs erected for him the first frame house ever built in Wisconsin. For nine years, he filled the office of Judge and performed his official duties, with a degree of promptitude and ability, that is astonishing to us of a later generation. Often alone and unattended, riding on an Indian pony, he traversed the length and breadth of the state, then a trackless and uninhabited wilderness, save by a few bands of nomadic Indians, whose friendship he always courted and never failed to win; He learned their language and always treated them with candor and respect.

In 1830, Congress made an appropriation for surveying and locating a military road from Green Bay to Chicago and thence to Prairie du Chien. Judge Doty and Lieut. Center of the U. S.

army were appointed Commissioners and surveyed and located these roads in 1831 and 1832.

In 1834 he was elected to the Legislative Council of the Territory of Michigan,—the seat of government being then at Detroit. It was while he was a member of that body, the question of a State Government was agitated, and he introduced the bill which finally prevailed.

In 1836, the Territory of Wisconsin was organized. General Dodge received the appointment of Governor, and assembled the first Legislature in the village of Belmont, now in Lafayette County. Judge Doty appeared there as a lobby member, having in his pocket a beautifully executed map of the Four Lakes country, where he had laid out in lots and blocks a city of magnificent proportions, and in its center a ten acre square, which he designated "Capitol Park," and in his pocket he had also a deed granting said park to the Territory for Capitol buildings. He worked quietly and effectively with the members, and when the matter came to a vote the seat of government was fixed at Madison, to the great disgust and astonishment of Gov. Dodge and the representatives of the lead region, then the most populous part of the Territory.

In 1838, Judge Doty was elected delegate to Congress and served till 1841, when he was appointed Governor of Wisconsin by President Tyler. While Governor and Superintendent of Indian affairs, the Indians in Minnesota began to be troublesome. The War Department appointed Gov. Doty as Commissioner to treat with them. He soon assembled the sachems and had a council. They listened with profound attention, difficulties were allayed and he made two highly important treaties which the Senate afterwards failed to confirm. In 1846, he was elected a member of the first Constitutional Convention, and in

1848 he was elected to Congress and re-elected in 1851. In 1853, he retired to his "Loggery" on Doty Island, and lived there uninterruptedly for the succeeding eight years. His wonted energies were now devoted to beautifying his home, and its surroundings. He enjoyed and maintained a very extensive correspond-ence. His library was a most interest-ing and unique museum, lined on all sides with books, public documents, In-dian implements of war, pipes, accou-trements, &c.; and here, with his most estimable and noble wife, he dispensed a genial and generous hospitality that made his home famous in other lands.

In the year 1861, President Lincoln appointed Gov. Doty, Superintendent of Indian Affairs for the Territory of Utah, and in the year following he was appointed Governor, which office he held up to the time of his death, which took place at Salt Lake City on the 13th day of June, 1865. He was interred at Camp Douglas cemetery, about four miles from the city, and there shortly af-terwards his son, Major Charles Doty, erected a massive granite monument to mark the last resting place of his hon-ored remains. No man in his day exer-cised a more potent influence in mould-ing the destinies of the state, and shap-ing its course than Gov. Doty, and his name will ever remain impressed upon the state as a memento of his useful, honorable and distinguished life.

EFFORTS TO CIVILIZE THE INDIANS.

The Menomonee Indians, having been always kindly disposed towards the whites, the general government in def-ference to a widely diffused sentiment of philantrophy, resolved to make an ef-fort to lead them gently into the ways of civilized life. To that end, in the year 1835, a settlement was started at Winnebago Rapids, now the site of the city of Neenah. A saw mill and a grist mill, as well as a large number of small neat dwelling houses' were erected by the agents of the government. A good blacksmith shop and carpenter shop were completely furnished, and an im-mense number of farming tools and im-plements were on hand, and all the able bodied Indians were requested to turn in and do an honest days work, and earn their bread. A few complied but the great body lounged around in listless idleness; and even those who were per-mitted to occupy the houses, instead of using chairs and tables and stoves, like the white people, secretly tore up the flooring and built fires in the center and then sat and slept around them as they were wont to do in their own bark wig-wams. In the morning many of them would start in and work with energy and alacrity, but before noon three-fourths of them would have thrown up their hoes and spades and retired to the shade. disheartened in their efforts to imitate the white man, and sighing for their ancient freedom and the peaceful gloom of the forest. They would beg that the great Father in Washington would pay them for the lands in this locality and move them back into the forest on to a reservation far away from the track and presence of the white man.

In 1833, the Indians, by treaty, sur-rendered all their right to all the land lying east of Fox River and Lake Win-nebago, and these lands were soon after-wards surveyed and put up for public sale at the Land Office in Green Bay. Money was plenty then. It was prev-ious to the great panic of 1837, when the country was flooded with paper mon-ey and the people were infatuated with a mania for speculation, and every per-son desired to secure for a small sum the site of a great future metropolis. Some choice sections, such as part of Doty Island sold as high as ten dollars an acre.

When the Indians got heartily sick of their experiments of civilization at Win-nebago Rapids, they sent a messenger to Washington to negotiate for a new location, and their abandonment of the Fox River Valley forever. Gov. Dodge was appointed a Commissioner to treat with them, and in due time he met them in a grand council at a point, where the city of Appleton is now located. It is said that Gov. Dodge, at the appointed moment, with much ceremony and in full dress, as a general of volunteers, and surrounded by a numerous suite, approached the dusky sachems and squaws, as if they were diplomatic courtiers from foreign lands. He made several long speeches to them, through his interpreter, and at intervals the Indians would give a grunt of satisfaction. And as the Gov. expatiated upon the power and grandeur of the United State government, and the great number and immense wealth of the white men, and how the great Father at Washington appointed him to speak to them in his place and stead, "And tell them" said he to the interpreter, "*that I am as great a man as Julius Caesar!*" The treaty made at this time resulted in the removal of the Menomonee Indians to their present reservation in Shawano County, and the extinguishment of the last remnant of the Indian title in this part of the state. This was in 1836, and the surveyors were immediately ordered to survey all the lands west of the Fox River and Lake Winnebego so that the same could be brought into market.

Gen. A. G. Ellis was then Surveyor General, and the lands in this neighborhood were surveyed by Garret Vleit under his supervision, in the year 1839. Gen. Ellis is now the only one of the pioneers of 1824 living. He is indeed the patriarch of Wisconsin—still active and useful, full of years and honors, he has served his generation to good purpose, and his name will live forever in the early annals of the state, as one of its most useful and honorable citizens. In his surveys of this section of the

country, Gen. Ellis was assisted by Col. Conkey, now a resident of this city.

After the Indians had abandoned the new settlement at Neenah, the government advertised the property for sale, together with several hundred acres of land. And Harrison Reid, who was then a printer on the *Milwaukee Sentinel*, without a dollar of capital at his command, made a tender of three thousand dollars for all the property both real and personal. This offer was accepted and Mr. Reid came on and took possession. Now his great object was to find some person with money enough to pay the government and share with him in the speculation. After a time he found out Harvey Jones in Gloverville, N. Y., who furnished the funds, and came west to enter upon the enterprise of starting a new town in the then wilderness. The name was now changed to Neenah, a Menomonee word, meaning *clear water*.

APPLETON.

Up to the year 1847, the site of the present city of Appleton reposed in all its primitive peace and beauty, unmarred by the woodman's axe and untenanted by savage or citizen. The great river rolled and tumbled over chute and rock, and swept on in its resistless course unfettered by dam or mill, and the high banks on either side were clothed with a luxuriant and varied vegetation. Here and there an opening studded with huge oaks and graceful elms, while in many places the thick underbrush, matted with vines and creepers, shut out the noonday sun, and completed a landscape as rare as it was beautiful.

The year previous the late Hon. Amos A. Lawrence made an offer to the Methodist Church of a donation of ten thousand dollars, provided a like amount would be raised by contribution for the purpose of establishing an educational institution on or near a tract of land he then owned near Depere. This land was low and uninviting, and being deemed unsuitable for that purpose, his offer was not accepted. But the following year he renewed his offer with liberty to locate the college on any part of the Lower Fox River, deemed most suitable. This offer was accepted, and a committee consisting of Reeder Smith, G. E. H. Day and H. L. Blood was appointed to select a site. After thorough search and examination, they decided to locate the institution here. In 1849, work was commenced on the first Institute building. It was a frame structure and was raised on the 3rd day of July, in that year, and on the following day, the Fourth was celebrated in and around it, John S. Stephens read the Declaration and Rev. A. B. Randall delivered the oration, and the Institute was opened the

following winter with thirty-five pupils. This building was burned down about the year 1853, and the present large and substantial structure was soon afterwards completed and occupied. The site of the present building was chosen by a lady in 1848, and she still lives here not ing with no small degree of interest the growth and progress of this great manufacturing city which clusters around it, and to the population of which it has always imparted, a moral and intellectual repute. Nearly all the first comers are still in the land of the living, and the story of their trials and struggles and triumphs remains for some future historian, after they shall have been called hence and the places that know them now shall know them no more forever.

FOX RIVER VALLEY.

APPLETON AS THE CENTRAL POINT.

TRANSPORTATION FACILITIES—IMPROVEMENTS—THE PLACE TO MANUFACTURE WOOLEN GOODS, IRON, COPPER AND LEAD—TIMBER RESOURCES—COTTON INDUSTRY—APPLETON AS A SUMMER RESORT—PARKS, DRIVES, SPORTING, ETC.—SCHOOLS, CHURCHES, ETC.

Appleton, a city of about eight thousand inhabitants, is situated on Fox River, five miles from Lake Winnebago, and twenty-nine miles from Green Bay. Its site is the most favorable, considering all things, in the Lower Fox River Valley, being for the most part situated on high table land which affords a commanding view of the river and its delightful scenery.

This valley embraces an area of about 1,280,000 acres—a tract of country lying between Lake Winnebago and Green Bay and including Winnebago, Outagamie, Calumet, and Brown Counties. The

whole of the territory included in this valley is excellent agricultural land, as fertile as that of any other equal portion of the State. The surface is gently undulating, and the soil of rich loam, capable of producing all kinds of cereals, vegetables and fruits, adapted to the 44th parallel of latitude. At present about three-fifths of this valley is under good cultivation, and the remainder is covered with a heavy growth of hard wood.

The river flows in a north-easterly course from Lake Winnebago to Green Bay where it finds an outlet. At various points in this portion of the river are natural falls and rapids which can be made available for gigantic manufacturing purposes. Nearly the whole length of the Lower Fox can be utilized by man for driving the wheels of machinery, and at a cost that prevents successful competition by factories run with artificial appliances.

That the reader may be better able to appreciate the advantages Appleton possesses for a manufacturing center, we subjoin a brief discussion of some of the prominent ones, and earnestly request a perusal of the same by all who are considering the advisability of engaging in manufacturing.

TRANSPORTATION.

As to transportation, its facilities are not surpassed by any manufacturing city in the West. The extensive farming districts of Southern Wisconsin, Illinois, and Minnesota, the lumbering and mining regions of Wisconsin and Upper Michigan are connected by a net work of railroads, and the Mississippi Valley and the Great Lakes are accessible through the instrumentality of the Government Canal which connects the Mississippi and Green Bay. Thus the whole Northwest becomes a market for all articles which can be manufactured here, through these various means of communication.

ADVANTAGES.

The advantages which Appleton possess over other localities for the investment of capital are of a pre-eminently superior character. Of the available points, Appleton is the only one which contains improved water-powers, with the many appliances and advantages which this necessarily implies. It does not require a large outlay of capital to build canals, dams, races, etc., to control the water before it can be used, for these with bridges, streets, accessible and convenient depots for shipment, have all been provided, leaving nothing of this nature to be done by those who locate

here. All that remains to be done is to select a suitable mill site (which can be purchased at a nominal price), and at once begin the construction of buildings. Those acquainted with the necessary improvements of a new locality, will at once recognize the desirability of locating where this work has been performed.

At present, the manufacturing interests include woolen goods, pig iron, wood pulp, paper, flour, barrel material, furniture, wagon material, sash and blinds, etc., etc.; but none of these is overdone, and there remains ample room for new factories of the same kind.

WOOL.

Those interested in the manufacture of woolen goods will at once recognize the superior advantages offered at Appleton. The manufacturers of the East labor under the disadvantage of double freight—the cost of transportation of wool to the East and of transportation of the manufactured goods to the West. Here this is obviated by bringing the consumer and producer into close proximity. The wool can be made into fabrics as cheaply here as in the most favored localities of the East, and as fine a quality of goods can be manufactured here as there. So far as the quantity of wool may enter into the feasibility, there is no question whatever. The best qualities of wool are grown in all the Northwestern States, and in quantities sufficient to stock factories of the largest capacity. Considerable attention has been given to wool growing in the Fox River Valley, during the past ten years, with great success, proving beyond a doubt that the best grades of wool can be grown here. With the increase of factories, the wool growers will become multiplied sufficiently to supply all demands of the manufacturer.

IRON.

By reference to a map, it will be seen at a glance that this is a favorable point for the manufacture of iron. The inexhaustible deposits of iron ore in the Lake Superior region are sufficient to supply the world for ages. The quality of the ore is nowhere surpassed, either on this or any other continent. It yields from 50 to 70 per cent. of that grade of iron which produces the best quality of steel. The Menomonee Iron Range, which is acknowledged by competent judges, to furnish the richest beds of ore, and the Penoke Iron Range are both favorably situated to Appleton, and each range is connected with it by railroads and the former by water communication. An able writer, in speaking of the manufacture of iron in the West, has said: In the matter of fuel we have only to say that our forests of hard wood have hardly been touched, and peat beds, in embryo, promise everything asked of them for the future; and when it becomes necessary, in the course of the next decade, to make a balance of lake freights heavier from the East to the West, we can load the lake crafts with coal to smelt our ores at home. If we bear in mind that charcoal iron is worth from five to ten dollars more per ton than that made with mineral coal, and also that the supply of timber, which can be easily converted into coal, is almost limitless, it will at once become apparent that the West is the proper place to manufacture these ores. During the great depression in business for the past five years, the Appleton blast furnace has been running constantly, while other furnaces which used mineral coal have been compelled to cease work. This can be accounted for only on the basis of a large saving in the manufacture of charcoal iron and the higher price it commands in the market. There is a wide field for capitalists to engage in the production of all kinds of articles, machinery, etc., for which iron is or may be used. The operations of foundries, machine shops, car works, rolling mills, cutlery factories, agricultural works, and

various other kinds of establishments for the utilization of this material, may be carried on with greater profit here than elsewhere. Many arguments might be put forth to show why this city is superior to any other in the Northwest for iron industries, but the following in addition to the above must suffice, viz.: all kinds of supplies used by operatives can be obtained here at a nominal price. These can be furnished at the very thresholds of factories at a much less cost than they can at points situated in a country poor in agricultural resources. In the iron districts scarcely any kind of food, except vegetables, can be raised profitably, and the cost of transporting supplies thither is a heavy drain on the manufacturer.

COPPER AND LEAD.

Copper and lead which are both found in large quantities in this State and adjoining States, can easily be obtained and manufactured here to advantage. Either or both of these industries would net a handsome return to those engaged in the business for the capital invested. There are no localities more favored than this for the manufacture of copper and lead, and hence there is no danger of being undersold by those engaged in the business elsewhere.

TIMBER.

Reference has already been made to the timber resources at our command. For the immediate present there is no business enterprise, perhaps, that can be engaged in here more profitably than that of utilizing the products of the forest. The belt of timbered country stretches away from Lake Michigan westward to the prairies of Minnesota, and from the great prairies of Northern Illinois and Southern Wisconsin to Lake Superior on the north. A large portion of this richly timbered country is now the haunts of wild beasts, or the home of Indian trappers. In this, as in the mineral resources of the Lake Superior

Region, nature has been lavish in her gifts, furnishing for the vast prairie country south and west a supply of timber for generations to come. Appleton lies within this timber belt; and all parts of this extensive forest have become accessible by rail and water communication. Thus it can be brought here easily and cheaply, and with the facilities of manufacturing, converted into various wares at a price which would challenge competition, and leave a large profit on the capital invested.

COTTON.

It now remains to present one other industry for which this city is pre-eminently fitted, but which has not, up to the present time, been introduced. That to which we now allude is the manufacture of cotton. Above attention has been called to the facilities of transportation, the supply of wood, the quantity of provisions and the extensive territory that is available for a market, and we desire to call the attention of the reader to these in connection with this topic that he may more fully comprehend the relation this city holds as a manufacturing center to the whole North-west. The feasibility of engaging in the manufacture of cotton will at once appear to those who are familiar with the advantage to be gained by bringing the consumer and producer together. This we claim for this city. There is no uncertainty about the supply of water or factory sites, as will be demonstrated in the next article. The cotton raised in at least one-half of the Southern States can be brought to the Fox River Valley at a much less cost than it can be transported to the Eastern States. A large portion of the cotton crop in the Mississippi Valley is shipped around the coast to various points convenient to the manufacturing towns, and at certain seasons of the year at great risk. Scarcely a season passes without the loss or damage of several cargoes, and the ex-

pense is again increased by extra insurance during the stormy weather of the fall and winter. The communication of this valley with the South is much shorter, more direct, and less expensive, owing to the comparative safety of inland over those of oceanic appliances of communication. At certain seasons of the year, cotton can be placed upon barges at favorable points along the Mississippi river, and without a transfer landed at the doors of the factories in Appleton. Aside from this, the railway routes are direct, penetrating the most favored cotton growing regions of the South.

The following gives approximately, the saving on the transportation of a ton of cotton, in favor of Appleton over Lowell, Mass., with Chicago as the distributing point:

From New Orleans to Boston, 2000 miles Ocean, at $.0025 per ton, per mile.............................$	5.00
Boston to Lowell, 26 miles, rail, at $.03 per ton, per mile..............$	.78
Lowell to Boston.......................$	.78
Boston to New York, 390 miles, Ocean, at $.0025 per ton, per mile $	.975
New York to Buffalo, 350 miles, canal, at $.006 per ton, per mile......$	2.100
Buffalo to Chicago, 1070 miles, Lake, $.004 per ton, per mile...........$	4.280
Total to Chicago.........$13.915	
New Orleans to Prairie du Chien, 1-786 miles, river, at $.0029 per ton, per mile..............................$	5.1794
Prairie du Chien to Appleton, 240 miles, canal, at $.007 per ton, per mile................................$	1.6800
Appleton to Green Bay, 35 miles, canal, at $.007 per ton, per mile.......$	.2450
Green Bay to Chicago. 310 miles, lake, at $.004 per ton, per mile....$	1.2400
Total to Chicago.........$ 8.3440	
Amount per ton in favor of Appleton.....................................$	5.571

The rates of transportation may vary somewhat from the above, but the distances are practically correct so that the difference of transportation would remain approximately as given above and in favor of Appleton. If railroad routes are compared it will be found that Appleton is a more favorable point than Lowell. The distance, by rail, from New Orleans to Lowell is 1710 miles and from Lowell to Chicago 994 miles, making an aggregate of 2704 miles. Again the distance from New Orleans to Appleton, by rail, is 1091 miles and from Appleton to Chicago 200 miles, making a total of 1291 miles, or a difference in favor of Appleton of 1413 miles. Allowing that the rates of transportation from New Orleans to Lowell, and from the former to Appleton are the same, it is evident that the latter takes precedence over Lowell. But cotton, to be manufactured here, can be obtained at points much nearer than New Orleans; for instance at Memphis, Tenn., which is still more favorable to this city, and in favor of this industry being conducted here.

It is a logical conclusion, therefore, from the above facts, that the manufacture of cotton fabrics with which to supply the West can be furnished here much cheaper than at the most favored localities of the East. It has been demonstrated by the Janesville cotton mills that this industry furnishes a safe investment, and returns a large profit to the manufacturer. In view of the foregoing it must appear to every candid mind that the manufacture of cotton goods in this Valley is not only feasible and practical, but that it is an enterprise which affords a safe and productive field of operation.

THE WEST.

In the West, during the past, manufacturing has not kept pace with the growth of agriculture. It is obvious to all why this should be so. From nearly all parts of the civilized globe, people have come to seek a home, being attracted by the liberality of the Government and the fertility of the soil. Upon arriving here, they soon discover that the tilling of the soil is the most profitable investment that can be made of their limited means. Hence, while the West is fast becoming the agricultural district of the world, the natural facilities for manufacturing are lying idle. From this standpoint, it will be seen at a glance

that there is every inducement for the investment of capital in the West, and at present no more favorable point than Appleton. With the lavish facilities nature has furnished us and the improvements man has added, this will eventually become the manufacturing center of the great North West.

SUMMER RESORT, ETC.,

But Appleton possesses other attractions than those of a manufacturing town. The Fox River Valley is noted for its health giving qualities. The climate is all that could be desired, being free from epidemic and miasmic diseases. The hot seasons are tempered with cool winds from the large bodies of lake water lying east and south; the winters are invigorating, being gently stimulating to the nerves, and bracing to the whole organization. The activity and enterprise of the inhabitants are sufficient in themselves to demonstrate the healthy state of the climate. As a summer resort, Appleton is one of the most favored in the State. The scenery along the river is picturesque and constantly varying. The sloping banks of the river, covered with a beautiful carpet of green or native forest trees; the ravines and glens at short intervals, full of nature's beauties; the woodland slopes and shady bowers with their never wearying surprises; the parks, with their groves of oak or maple and beach, all unite and blend in perfect harmony to make this city an attractive place to live. It is not surpassed for its many delightful drives into the country, or points of interest to visit by pleasure parties. At the western extremity of the city is Pierce's Park which is situated on an elevated plateau overlooking the river. It has been kept in its natural state, and is quite a favorite place of resort for picnic parties and lovers of boating. At the eastern extremity is Telulah Park. This park contains about twenty-five acres in all, and is covered with a natural growth of

TELULAH MINERAL SPRINGS.

See page 16

hard wood. The principal entrance into the park runs along the river bank, close to the water's edge, thus forming a novel and pleasant drive. At the end of this drive is situated the well known Telulah springs. The water of these springs, which is crystal clear, pours from the hillside into reservoirs about ten feet above the river. The capacity of the springs is nearly six thousand gallons per day. Gustave Bode, analytical chemist of Milwaukee, found by analysis that the water of these springs contains the same salts in about the same proportion as that of the Bethesda springs of Waukesha, and like that has wonderful curative efficiency in Bright's disease, diabetes, kidney affections, dropsy, etc., etc. The springs lie just beyond the foot of Grand Chute rapids, and its site is pleasant and delightful. Terrace drives lead from the springs to the top of the hill where a fine race course has been constructed. This is situated in a grove of native maple, and has already become the resort of lovers of the turf. No more charming spot can be found in Fox River Valley for a summer house than this park. The river abounds in fish, the woods in small game, and the rice marshes along the river in wild duck. It is here that the sportsman can find a home—a field in which to pursue his wonted pastime. The Educational advantages are no where surpassed in the West. It is the seat of Lawrence University—a college conducted by the M. E. Church for the education of both sexes. It has an excellent corps of instructors who are devoted to their work. The public schools are being rapidly improved, and to-day they rank high with similar institutions of larger and more pretentious cities. The churches are all in a flourishing condition, and hence the morality of the town ranks high. The people are intelligent and cultivated. Its homes are pleasant and cheerful. The hospitality of the citizens has become proverbial, and every attention that could be wished by those who visit here will be extended to them.

FOX AND WIS. RIVER IMPROVEMENT.

THE IMPORTANCE OF THE GREAT NATURAL ROUTE, CONNECTING THE WEST WITH THE SEABOARD—A BRIEF HISTORY OF THE ENTERPRISE FROM ITS INCEPTION, DOWN TO THE PRESENT TIME—THE VARIOUS ADMINISTRATIONS WHICH HAVE HAD CHARGE OF THE WORK—WHAT HAS BEEN ACCOMPLISHED AND THE PRESENT CONDITION OF THE ROUTE—HINTS AS TO WHAT IT WILL ACCOMPLISH FOR THE INDUSTRIAL CLASSES OF THE COUNTRY.

This is the connecting link of a great international highway. Commencing in the Gulf of St. Lawrence, it traverses the eastern boundary of the Dominion of Canada, thence making a circuit of the great lakes, it enters the Fox River at Green Bay, thence into the Wisconsin and down to the Mississippi; and after traversing four thousand miles through the interior of the continent, it finds its exit in the Gulf of Mexico. A more important water highway does not exist on the face of the globe. From beginning to end, all along every mile of the route, the country is luxuriant and fruitful, and inhabited by an industrious, intelligent and prosperous people. The commerce of the lakes of late years has assumed immense proportions. The money invested in vessels and steamers is counted by the hundreds of thousands, and the commerce of the lakes every year adds greatly to the wealth of the nation. The floating commerce of the Mississippi is also extensive, and would be much increased could its steamers and vessels ascend into the great lakes, laden with the fruits and valuable productions of the South, and there exchange them for the rich minerals and productions of the North, thus helping to bind with the peaceful bands of commerce the extreme sections of the nation. But the improvement of the "connecting link," to such an extent is considered by many impractical, if not impossible. This may or may not be the correct view of the subject. With that we have nothing to do in this connection. In any event however, the streams connecting the Mississippi with the lakes can be improved to an extent which will prove of great and permanent advantage to the nation. The great importance of this highway has been heretofore underestimated. It has been looked upon as a local enterprise, benefiting only the immediate locality in which money was to be expended. This was the spirit that led to its abandonment by the State, and the surrender of the valuable land grant of the Government to the Fox and Wisconsin Improvement Company, in the year 1853. The few individuals who carried the burdens of this latter company, acted with great energy and enterprise and, in the summer of 1856, the improvement was opened, and vessels drawing two or three feet of water could pass through from the lakes to the Mississippi. This was a great triumph for The Fox and Wisconsin River Improvement Company and also for the people of the State. The original grant to the State for this improvement embraced 318,720 acres of land, but the State, during the years it

carried on the improvement, received only 131,600 acres.

The lands remaining unsold in 1853, and which were granted to the Fox and Wisconsin River Improvement Company by the terms of its charter, amounted to about 168,000 acres which were valued at about $800,000.

In 1854, an act of Congress was passed authorizing the Governor to select the balance of the grant of 1846, to which the State was entitled and provided how the quantity of land should be ascertained.

After the passage of this resolution the Commissioner of the General Land Office issued a certificate to the Governor of the State, authorizing the selection of 415,134 acres. In 1856, the State granted to the Company these lands on the conditions mentioned in Chapter 112, general laws of 156.

Thus, it will be seen that the general government granted to the State of Wisconsin more than seven hundred thousand acres of land, worth at least $2,000,000, to help towards the opening of this great highway.

In 1866, The Fox and Wisconsin Improvement Company, its franchises, grants and effects, were sold out under a decree of the Circuit Court of Fond du Lac County. The sale took place in the city of Appleton, and the "Improvement" became the property of the Green Bay and Mississippi Canal Company.

This corporation owned this great water route and continued to operate it until 1872. For some time previous to this date, however, the leading men of Wisconsin, Minnesota, Iowa and other Western States, appreciating the great service which this water way was adapted to perform for the industrial and agricultural interests of the Great West, and indirectly for the whole country, had been advocating the policy and wisdom of the government taking hold of the enterprise. They argued wisely and well that the grand results accomplished by the Erie Canal, to-wit: the saving in freights to the people of the country during a single decade, reaching from 1855 to 1864, of $123,000,000, could again be repeated, in our day, by opening up this route to the internal commerce of the nation. And they further argued that in order to secure to the people the full benefits in the way of cheap transportation which would be sure to follow the consummation of the improvement, the government should take hold of the matter: first, because of the magnitude of the undertaking and, secondly, because that, in order to secure the results mentioned to the people, it should be made simply a self-sustaining route rather than a money-making enterprise. The effort thus put forth was brought to a successful issue and at the time stated, this great water route, together with all of the navigable franchises, was transferred to the government.

The work of improving the rivers was then inaugurated by the government and on a scale commensurate with their great importance. Liberal appropriations have been made thus far and will probably be continued until the work is accomplished. The following are the amounts expended by the government:

Purchase price........................$145,000
1873 appropriation.................... 300,000
1874   "   300,000
1875   "   500,000
1876   "   270,000

    Total............... ....$1,515,000

We believe the appropriations, thus far, have been utilized to the best possible advantage. Of course a considerable amount of repairs was necessary but it has been the policy of the engineers in charge to invest the public funds in new and permanent work.

But little has been expended upon the Wisconsin River as yet, first, because the plan of permanently improving it is, as yet, immature, and, secondly, because it is impracticable to prose-

cute the work of improvement upon such a great extent of route at the same time.

Upon the Upper and Lower Fox, however, a fine work has been accomplished. And it is in order here to detail somewhat the improvements made. Upon the former section of the river, stone locks and dams have been built at Eureka, Berlin, Grand River, Princeton and White River. This work is all of the most permanent character and will never have to be rebuilt.

On the Lower river, a very large amount of work has been done. We particularize the new work accomplished up to and during the year 1877: a stone dam at Appleton, a combined stone lock at Little Chute; a stone lock at Appleton; another combined stone lock at Little Chute; two stone locks at Kaukauna—known as the 3d and 5th; dams have also been constructed at Cedars, Little Chute, Kaukauna, Rapid Croshe and Little Kaukauna.

During the past year, this section of the river has been the scene of active and extensive operations. The most important undertaking was the construction of a new crib dam at Depere, 1,400 feet in length. The banks of the canal have also been raised at Menasha, Appleton, Kaukauna and Depere. And sections of the river that required it, between the points first and last mentioned, have been thoroughly dredged. Some of the work of previous years has this season been completed—principally the surmounting of various locks along the stream with stone coping. The lower dam, in this city, has been thoroughly repaired and placed in a condition to perform good service for quite a number of years. A number of old locks have likewise been overhauled. New miter cills and gates have been put in and a variety of other necessary work has been performed. A large force of hands has been employed. and their operations will be continued through the winter, quarrying and cutting stone for new locks to be constructed hereafter.

The various operations first inaugurated necessitated the closing of the river to navigation until the commencement of the season of '77. But during the past two years the route has been opened the entire length and will continue to remain so hereafter during the season of navigation. And the extent to which it has been utilized in the period mentioned indicates the importance of the route and argues well for the future.

The present condition of the channel is most satisfactory. A uniform depth of 5 feet and 4 inches has been secured the entire length, and at no time, during the past year, even at the lowest stage of water, was its capacity less than this.

While it is true that the importance of this route to Appleton and adjacent towns is manifest and very great, it is also of the utmost consequence to the producing classes of the great West and to the consumers of the East as well. It has been computed by high congressional authority that the improvement of the great water way between the Mississippi and the Lakes, to an extent which is entirely practicable and the subsequent utilizing of it as a line of transportation would save to the people of this country $60,000,000 every year. These figures may appear extravigant but it is not for us to dispute the estimate which was submitted by the Transportation Committee, after a thorough investigation of the facts. The statement certainly has some justification in the well known results secured by the construction and operation of the Erie Canal —the aggregate saving, as submitted by good authority, being over $300,-000,000. The improvement of the Fox and Wisconsin Rivers is simply an extension of the Erie Canal, only on a grander scale, to the Mississippi River. And the country which the former route is to serve is vastly greater in extent and more productive than the territory tributary to the latter, when that famous channel was constructed.

But it is needless for us to dwell further upon the importance of this great enterprise. That is generally admitted, and, as has been seen in the foregoing, a considerable start has already been made in the way of improving these rivers— enough at least to fully commit the government to the undertaking and to secure the completion of the work in the near future. But even if large investments had not already been made for this purpose there is enough of merit in this water way to secure for it the preference over all other similar lines. It is by far the shortest of any of the water routes connecting the Great West with the sea board, and as the result of careful investigation and comparative estimates, it has been ascertained that its improvement can be accomplished at much less expense. There is nothing, therefore, to stand in the way of the opening up of these rivers, on an extensive scale, to the commerce of the nation.

THE LOWER FOX RIVER.

ONE OF THE GREATEST SOURCES OF NATURAL POWER ON THE CONTINENT—INDEED, ALL
THINGS CONSIDERED, THERE IS NOTHING OF THE KIND WHICH COMPARES WITH IT—
SOME OF ITS SALIENT FEATURES REVIEWED IN THIS CONNECTION—PARTICULAR AL-
LUSION TO ITS NATURAL SUPERIORITY AND THE IMPROVEMENTS WHICH HAVE SERVED
TO INCREASE ITS AVAILABILITY.

THE FOX RIVER WATER POWER.

There is not another stream in the western hemisphere which affords as great power within a given space, and which is so reliable, thoroughly available and easily controlled, as the Lower Fox River. Before, however, proceeding to treat the details of our subject, as regards Appleton, with which we have especially to do, we may as well submit, for the consideration of the reader who may be a stranger to this section, the figures, showing the extent of power which the Lower Fox River affords in this Valley, in its course of less than 40 miles. Competent engineers have placed them as follows and they have been amply verified by subsequent calculations. The height and power of water falls, on the Lower Fox, between the points first and last mentioned, a distance of less than 40 miles, is as follows:

Names of places.	Feet fall.	Horse-power.
Neenah and Menasha....	10	3,000
Appleton..................	38	11,500
Cedars....................	10	3,000
Little Chute...............	38	11,500
Kaukauna.................	40	14,500
Rapid Crosche............	8	2,300
Little Kaukauna..........	8	2,300
Depere...................	8	2,300
Total..............	150	50,400

But it is pertinent to remark that this statement of facts does not represent the power afforded by the greatest flowage. They express the quantity of power created by the flowage of water, at its very lowest stage. Hence, as all calculations are made upon this basis, there need be no fear, even when its fullest capacity is utilized, that the requirements of any industry need be re-

strained on account of the inadequate supply.

While it is a fact, as will be seen by consulting the above figures that other contiguous points are highly favored, it is nevertheless true that at Appleton are combined more advantages than are possessed at any other point. At Neenah, Menasha, and Depere, the available power is almost entirely utilized; or at least there is not enough left to attract any very important industries. The aggregate, as will be seen, is much less at either or all of these places, than the river at Appleton affords. And at other points, where the natural power is even greater, but few if any improvements have been made to add to its availability. At Appleton, as will be seen, in what follows, the situation is quite different. Here everything has been done, in the way of material improvements which labor could perform or money secure, to make the natural power afforded by the river highly servicable. The manufacturer who locates here now, therefore is relieved from the burdens which would be placed upon him in more primitive localities and which his predecessors here also had to bear.

But we must dismiss these considerations for the more important work in hand, viz., that of submitting such facts and figures as that the wonderful power at Appleton may be comprehended and appreciated by those who are not familiar with it from personal observation.

CAPACITY.

As indicated in the general table,

above submitted, the water power at Appleton is equivalent to that exerted by 11,500 horses. A passing glance bestowed upon these figures will not meet the expectation of the writer hereof. And to have their importance fully understood they should receive careful consideration by the reader. If the same power were invested in perishable bone and muscle, the fortune of the town possessing it would be the source of general envy. But, in that form, the exerting of so much power, would imply a large annual consumption. In the case of Appleton it is different. All that is required is the harness to secure from this wonderful agent the vast power which it is competent to exert. Notwithstanding the considerable amount which is already employed there is yet water enough running to waste through Appleton to drive all of the machinery in the largest New England town.

RELIABILITY.

This is the strong point that we never omit to urge in connection with the Appleton water power. The supply of water in the Fox River is not drawn from mountain torrents but is primarily made up from numberless tributaries, ramifying a vast expanse of slightly undulating territory. In addition to this, at the head of the Lower Fox and upon some of its confluent streams, are numerous lakes or natural reservoirs which, combined, have an immense area. For example, Lake Winnebago alone is 40 miles long and has an average width of at least 12 miles. These lakes receive the discharges from the upper streams and have sufficient capacity to contain the accumulations for months together. The result is that the water powers on the lower stream are absolutely independent of both droughts and freshets. The flowage is very uniform and the difference between high and low water mark is never greater than 30 inches. We need not suggest the benefit of this

natural arrangement to manufacturers less favorably located, many of whom have had the accumulations of a life time swept away in a single night, and others who are obliged to limit or entirely suspend their operations, two or three months in every year, for the want of adequate power.

We have before us an elaborate and handsomely executed publication, devoted to the city of Holyoke, Mass., and its great water power on the Connecticut River. The supply of this river, like that of most of the New England streams, proceeds from a mountainous country and the fluctuations are, therefore, wonderful in extent—indeed sufficient to destroy all of the property located upon it were it not for the ingeniously artificial means employed to regulate it. In one of the illustrations which has arrested our attention, we notice that the machinery required for this purpose is great in extent, very complicated and expensive. Moreover, men are employed, day and night, year in and year out, to manipulate it and regulate the flow of water—thus guarding against the dangers arising from sudden and great fluctuations. Upon the Lower Fox, nature performs all of this labor and with a care and precision which are nowhere equalled. And it is by reason of these natural characteristics that the water power at Appleton is superior to that at other points and with the same demand can be afforded so much cheaper, because the cost of controlling and maintaining it is vastly less than upon any other stream.

ANOTHER POINT OF IMPORTANCE.

It is worthy of remark, in this connection, that the extreme rigor of our northern climate, during the winter season, in no way interferes with the driving of machinery. Block ice is never created in such quantities as to cause disturbance or create irregularity in the activity of industrial enterprises. For how few water powers in the same latitude of Appleton can this claim truthfully be made?

AVAILABILITY.

That this is a feature of great consequence will be so recieved without argument. Indeed a great power would be of little value, if the advantages did not exist to control and utilize it. Steam had as great power previous to as after its discovery, and even after its usefulness was known, it would have been of little consequence unless devices had been constructed to make it servicable. So with water. It would be difficult to comprehend the power of Niagaria, but still it is of little account to human industry. The reason, of course, is that it lacks in the essential feature of availability. But that is what the power at Appleton possesses in a pre-eminent degree.

For the purpose of enabling the reader to comprehend more readily what we have to say, we herewith submit the accompanying map. (Since this map was executed, a new dam has been constructed above the upper bridge which will be noticed hereafter; also the proposed route of the W. C. R. R. has been somewhat changed and the M. L. S. & W. R. R., has been extended across the river, touching the bank near the upper flouring mills.

In his tracing of the map, the reader is invited to assume as the initial point of the examination, that section of the river which is divided by the upper or stone dam. This magnificient structure is the work of the government for the improvement of navigation upon the Lower Fox. It was built in the summer of 1874, at a total cost of $50,000. It is 700 feet long, 12 feet high, and is built of solid stone masonry. It is by far the most enduring structure of the kind on the line of the river, and, in fact, no better or more substantial one could be built. Besides answering the purpose of the government, it will also serve as a permanent improvement to the water power facilities of this place. As will be seen, a considerable portion of the waters flowing in the main channel is directed, by means of the stone dam and the adjacent pier on the south side, into the canal originally the property of the Green Bay and Micsissippi Canal Co., but afterwards purchased by the government. The primary object of this artificial channel is to subserve the purposes of navigation, but the supply of water is so abundant that the demands of commerce may be met, besides leaving a residue of ample magnitude to be utilized in driving machinery of various kinds. Accordingly, this canal may be tapped on either side, at any point, and any amount of water may be drawn therefrom that may be desired. It will be noticed that the length of the upper level is 1800 feet: that the middle level 1,700 feet; and that of the lower level 2,600 feet. The reader will observe that a series of water-powers can be furnished by this channel for a distance of over one mile, with an avarage head of not less than 13 feet. A canal may also be extended several hundred feet below the point where the lower lock is situated, and a series of magnificent water-powers thus be created. The owners of the land in this vicinity already have such an improvement in contemplation.

On either side of the government canal are spacious accommodations for factory sites, the greater part of the distance. The water-power franchises created by this canal, are still in the possession and at the disposal of the Green Bay and Mississippi Canal Company, by which they were retained when the balance of the property was disposed of to the government. The depth of this canal is seven feet, and the average width 130 feet.

There are contained in this Annual

Review of the Post cuts appropriately illustrating the upper and lower levels of this canal and to which the attention of the reader is invited for more definite information on the subject. Therein are represented certain contemplated improvements which will be made as the utilization of other powers proceeds and the rapidly growing demands of the place warrants them. The most excellent water power privileges have been and can now be leased from the G. B. & M. C. Co., at rates which are simply nominal, compared with the prevailing rates elsewhere. Indeed we may as well submit the astonishing figures in this connection, to-wit: from $1 to $5 per horse power per year, for a long term of years. Parties locating upon the banks of this channel secure with other advantages the most convenient facilities for transportation by water to all of the principal markets of the east, as well as the more important intermediate points.

On the north side of the river similar advantages exist, and indeed some of the best powers in the city are to be found on this side of the river, contiguous to the stone dam. A very important work has been accomplished, this year, in enlarging and improving these powers, and to which particular allusion is made a little farther on.

LATE IMPORTANT IMPROVEMENTS.

During the summer of 1877, a fine work was accomplished on the river at this point, viz.: the construction of a permanent dam, across the river at a point corresponding with the central part of the city. The utility of such a work had long been recognized. Accordingly a company was organized, under the state laws, to proceed with the undertaking. It is composed of manufacturers and property owners, on the river, specially interested and also of quite a large number of our business men who gave substantial aid to the un-

dertaking. Plans were presented and adopted and the work of construction was at once proceeded with under the supervision of Capt. N. M. Edwards. The undertaking was accomplished early the same season and at a cost of $10,000. The dam is 800 feet long and is so firmly and securely constructed, as to be safe, durable and permanent. The plan adopted to regulate the flow of water at this point is ingenious and admirable, and the tests to which it has already been submitted have proved that it is also eminently practical. The water way is limited to 440 feet and by the system of diminishing it and increasing it to this extent has proved to be the very thing required. A uniform head is thus preserved and one that varies but a trifle the year through.

The great utility of this dam is that it makes permanent, in the heart of our city, a magnificent series of powers, which had hitherto depended on treacherous and temporary structures. And, indeed, it was one of the few important undertakings required to render forever secure and make available, to the fullest extent, the means with which nature has provided us to carry on great industrial operations.

THIS YEAR.

A very important work has been accomplished, during the summer of 1878, calculated to perfect our admirable sys- of powers as well as to add to their great capacity. We may first allude to the improvements which have been made on the upper power, on the north side of the river, near the stone dam. This was the joint work of the Appleton Paper and Pulp Co., Col. Theo. Conkey and the Atlas Paper Co. This channel has been broadened and deepened so that its capacity is fully three or four times as great as heretofore. Several sections of the structure, dividing this channel from the river have also been rebuilt this season—making the entire pier, reach-

DATA

POWER.

NT IMPROVEMENTS, IS RE

THE BADGER BROADCAST SEEDER AND CULTIVATOR COMBINED.

OUR NEW PATENT TOOTH

AND

IMPROVED LIFTER

far excel all others
in

SIMPLICITY and DURABILITY

OUR NEW

SOWING DEVICE

HAS NO EQUAL

by means of which

FINE   COARSE GRAIN

can be

Sown more Perfect Account

— AND —

without fear of becoming clogged with straw or dirty grain.

We guarantee the Badger to perform as good or better work than any other machine in the market. All we ask is that it may be tried.

We manufacture the celebrated Horse-hoe Cultivator which is without a successful competitor, and the Land & Peck-skill Plows, which are known for their merits the world over. We also manufacture and deal in a variety of other machinery and implements, and can supply any want of the farming community.

Appleton M'f'g Co.

WITH IMPORTANT IMPROVEMENTS, IS READY FOR THE FARMERS.

SKETCH AND DATA

OF THE

APPLETON WATER POWER.

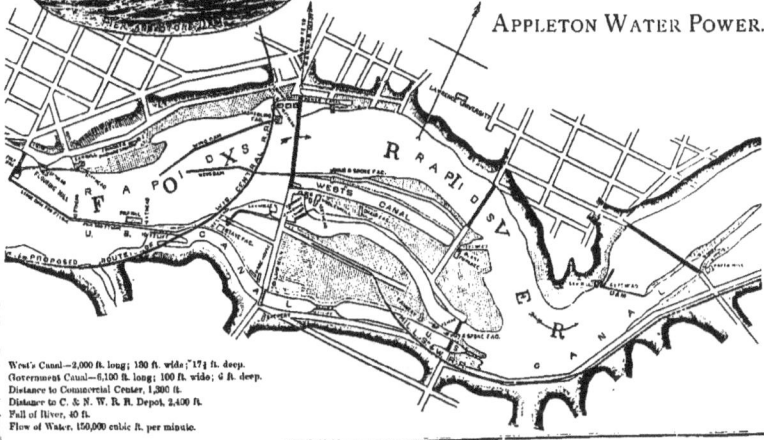

West's Canal—2,000 ft. long; 130 ft. wide; 17½ ft. deep.
Government Canal—6,100 ft. long; 100 ft. wide; 6 ft. deep.
Distance to Commercial Center, 1,300 ft.
Distance to C. & N. W. R. R. Depot, 2,400 ft.
Fall of River, 40 ft.
Flow of Water, 150,000 cubic ft. per minute.

We guarantee the BADGER to perform as good or better work than any other machine in the market. All we ask is that it may be tried.

We manufacture the celebrated horse-hoe Cultivator which is without a successful competitor, and the Lord & Peekskill Plows, which are known for their merits the world over. We also manufacture and deal in a variety of other machinery and implements, and can supply any want of the farming community.

APPLETON M'F'G Co.

ADY FOR THE FARMERS.

ing from the north end of the stone dam to the Atlas Paper Mills of the most durable and permanent character. The series of water powers in this vicinity are among the best to be found anywhere. The average head is fully 16 feet and the supply of water is limited only to the capacity of the river. That they are fully appreciated is seen from the large amount of capital now employed in manufacturing at that point.

The great bulk of the flowage of the river, however, passes over the stone dam and down the principal stream. At a distance of about 1,400 feet from this point, the current of the river is divided by Grand Chute Island. Through this island, several years ago, Mr. Edward West built a ship canal and created magnificent water privileges which are minutely described elsewhere.

THE LOWER POWER.

Below the eastern terminus of West's canal is another dam, about 10 feet in height, by means of which another series of magnificent water-powers can be created. Some of this power is already utilized, but the great bulk of it is still unappropriated. On the east side a canal may be extended to any desired distance, from which power may be drawn. This is one of the improvements which is already contemplated, by the owners of the land adjoining, and will doubtless be undertaken and accomplished within a very few years.

On the west side of the river a very important work has been accomplished this season, although it was not undertaken until quite late. We allude to the canal which has been constructed by Messrs Heath & Bro., and which taps the main river a little distance above the lower dam. This channel which has an average width of 25 feet reachs down stream 840 feet and upon the river side has been created some fine water sites and privileges for manufacturing purposes. The Dickerson Shutter Works

and the new grist mill, constructed this season, will derive their power directly from this source. But there is still room enough left for several other factories in that vicinity.

WHAT HAS ALREADY BEEN DONE.

It is with a good deal of pride that we refer, briefly in this connection, to what has already been accomplished in utilizing the water-powers of the Lower Fox at this place. Indeed the capital already invested upon the river is counted by the millions. And during the past two years especially a great deal has been accomplished, as is fully set forth upon other pages. This fact has a peculiar significance, when the point is kept in mind that most other towns have been retrograding. The only adequate explanation which can be offered is that the superior advantages which Appleton enjoys are becoming known and appreciated; and that men of means have wisely concluded that, by investing their capital here, it can be made to yield a much larger revenue than at other points or than it can command in the way of interest.

WHAT OF THE FUTURE?

That is a question which interests us most now. Of course that the utilizing of these great advantages will proceed is apparent, reasoning from the past. And that this process will be a rapid one is a rational conclusion, so long as men of wisdom and far-reaching vision exist. As we have shown the places are few in this or any other country which possess the facilities which Appleton enjoys for manufacturing on an extensive scale; and to say that these will not, sooner or later, be utilized to the fullest extent is to assume that human stagnation will overtake the race.

NOW!

No better time can exist than the present for men of means, not now actively engaged, to be casting about for a location. The time is not far distant when there will be a general revival in industrial operations; and when it comes those who are prepared for it will be the winners. Appleton, as we have shown, posseses advantages that are unrivalled. The best of power can be leased or purchased at merely nominal rates, and the materials for manufacture are within easy reach and can be had in endless quantities. And, in a thousand other ways, Appleton, as in the past, extends an earnest and cordial invitation to come.

OUR MANUFACTURING INDUSTRIES.

NOTWITHSTANDING THE "HARD TIMES," WE ARE ABLE TO PRESENT A VERY GRATIFYING EXHIBIT OF THE OPERATIONS FOR '78—BY WHICH IT APPEARS THAT THERE HAS BEEN A CONSIDERABLE INCREASE IN THE PRODUCT—NEW AND MAMMOTH ESTABLISHMENTS ERECTED AND THE OLD ONES ENLARGED AND IMPROVED—THE VARIOUS CONCERNS NOW IN OPERATION SOMEWHAT PARTICULARLY REVIEWED.

INTRODUCTORY COMMENTS.

As a manufacturing center the city of Appleton occupies an enviable rank among western towns. And the reader who is anxious to ascertain the reason why will find ample facts and figures for his enlightenment upon these pages. That this city, with its wonderful and superior natural advantages, is calculated to achieve far greater distinction, in this respect, in the near future, is as certain as that effect follows cause. The past year has witnessed immense strides, in the development of our manufacturing interests. And considering that this has been accomplished at a time before the business of the country has been released from the universal depression which has prevailed during the past five years, the progress made has a peculiar and telling significance. The adequate explanation may be briefly stated by submitting the potential fact that few if any towns in the whole country can present the inducements for the investment of large capital in manufacturing industries which the city of Appleton possesses.

PAPER AND PULP MILLS.

There are but few places in the whole country, so thoroughly adapted to this important industry as the city of Appleton. But a very few years have elapsed since any considerable start was made in this direction, but even the intervening short period has sufficed to place the city a long way ahead of any town in the state, in this respect, and we believe there are none in the west which surpass Appleton as a paper manufacturing center. The cause of this wonderful progress is obvious. Here there is plenty of pure water, so essential to the manufacture of this class of goods; ample and convenient facilities for transportation and at the lowest rates, by land and water; and what is of the greatest importance of all—an abundance of natural power which can be secured at prices that constitute but an inconsiderable item in the construction account of any establishment. As will be seen, in the subsequent comments, the year 1878 has been a very important one for Appleton, so far as the development of the paper industry is concerned.

THE ATLAS PAPER MILLS.

This is the largest establishment of the kind in the West and there are none in the whole country having greater capacity. It has been in operation but a couple of months, having been constructed during the past season. The site occupied by these mills is one of the very best in the city, it being the same as that on which Whorton Bro's. saw mill was formerly situated. There is all the yard room required and the power is unvarying and absolutely unlimited. One of the franchies secured by the company calls for 500 horse power—probably one third more than even this mammoth concern will ever require. The buildings are immense. The upright part is 75x140 feet and the machine room is 90x120 feet. The latter is two and the former three stories high. The buildings are of the most substantial and desirable character. The foundation is of stone and the superstructure is brick. The whole is covered with an iron roof —making the establishment practically fire proof, at least so far as outside exposures are concerned. The machinery of this concern is of the very best and highly improved kind that could be procured for this purpose and throughout is the product of the Merrill & Houston Iron Co. of Beloit. The principal items under this head are one large 78 inch Fourdrinier, with 36 feet of wire, one 68 inch thribble cylinder and one 68 inch double cylinder and twelve 600 pound beating engines. In addition there are of course all of the appliances necessary for the manufacture of paper on an extensive scale and economical basis. To make the Atlas Paper Mills the complete establishment which they are to-day has involved an outlay of $125,000. But in the hands of the energetic and experienced corporation which own and control it, there is no doubt that it will prove a paying and highly satisfactory investment.

Although the machinery is adapted to the manufacture of any grade of paper, the product is at present and will probably continue to be exclusively manilla wrapping paper and manilla goods in general. The material used to secure this result is pulp made from pine wood, in the manner to be hereafter noticed, and jute a vegetable matter imported from the East Indies. Of the former from 50 to 75 per cent is used, according to the particular grade required. The quality of these goods is most excellent and will compare favorably with the best of the kind in the market. The fact is that they have found easy, swift and general introduction to the paper trade is the best proof that can be offered on this point. The capacity of this establishment is from 10 to 12 tons per day. Reckoning the price at 5 cts. per pound, which is probably as low as it will ever be, and we find that the value of the daily product would be from $1,000 to $1,200 per day, or about $325,-000 annually.

To do this labor requires a force of 60 hands—many of whom are workmen of skill and experience. From the above figures, an accurate idea may be had of the magnitude of this industry.

The Atlas Paper Co. is a stock corporation, organized under the general laws of the state. The corporators are Messrs. Kimberly, Clark, Shattuck and Babcock of Neenah and Gen. Averill, Col. Stowell, H. M. Carpenter and Mr. Wilder of Minnesota. The company is officered as follows :

President.—Gen. Averill.

Vice Presidents.—Messrs. Kimberly and Carpenter.

Secretary and Treasurer.—Col. Stowell.

General Manager.—C. B. Clark.

The company is one of the strongest, financially, in the West. And the men who compose it have had large experience in the paper business and are lead-

ers in this particular industry. That
their magnificent enterprise in Appleton
will prove even more profitable than any
other of their important undertakings,
neither we nor they have any doubt.

THE ATLAS CO'S PULP MILLS.

As already intimated this establishment is operated in conjunction with
the paper mills, above mentioned, and is
also the property of the company named.
It was erected during the season of 1877
and is one of the most complete pulp
mills in the country. It is located near
the government pier, in the Fourth
Ward, and is connected with the company's paper mills, by a bridge on the
opposite side of the river. The wood
which this establishment converts into
pulp is pine exclusively. The process
of grinding is the same as that used in
the other mills, but before this is done
the wood is thoroughly cooked or steam-
ed. This gives a better and stronger
fiber than can otherwise be obtained.
This plan is a new one, but it has already
been thoroughly tested and with results
which leave no doubt as to its permanent success. The pulp product, thus
obtained, is the very best as well as
being the most economical material that
can be utilized in the manufacture of
wrapping paper. The establishment
named employs a force of 35 hands and
the sales for the year 1878 aggregate to
$60,000.

THE APPLETON PAPER AND PULP MILLS.

The business of manufacturing wood
pulp, by this company was commenced
about five years ago, but the establishment of to-day possesses scarcely a single feature of what distinguished it in
its earlier history. First the old method
of making pulp was discarded on account of its not proving entirely satisfactory to the proprietors. Accordingly
this machinery was removed and the
necessary facilities introduced for the
manufacture of print paper. The building was more than doubled in size and a

complete outfit of new machinery was
put in.

Since then, this branch of the business has been conducted on a large
scale. The paper manufactured cannot
be excelled in quality. It is now being
used by many of the largest newspapers
in the west, and that it fully meets the
wants of consumers is seen in the fact
that the full capacity of the mills is
tested in filling the orders which are
constantly being received. In the manufacture of this paper the best class of
machinery is used, which gives to the
sheet greater strength and uniformity
than can be secured from inferior facilities.

During the year 1877 a pulp manufacturing department was added.
The building was again enlarged and
new and superior facilites for grinding
wood were introduced. Of course, as
our readers know, the pulp thus obtained constitutes one of the ingredi-
ents used in the manufacture of paper.
When combined with rag pulp, in proportions varying from 10 to 40 per cent.,
an excellent quality of paper is obtained
and at less cost than otherwise attends
its production .

During the past season this Company
has made numerous important improvements and indeed these are still in progress. It has aided materly in improving the water power in that vicinity and on its own account has rebuilt
portions of the dam or pier in a more
permanent and substantial manner.
The channel, in front of the mills, has
been planked over and a great deal of
valuable room has thus been acquired,
This platform has been extended to
some extent above the mill so as to create fine dock privileges which will prove
of great importance. The old boiler
house and contents have been entirely
removed and a fire proof structure has
been erected and new and larger boilers
have been put in. A ware house has

also been erected, at a convenient distance from the mill, of ample dimensions to accommodate manufactured. goods and the raw materials always required. This is situated alongside the railroad track and is therefore as convenient as could be desired. But the most important improvement is now in progress, by which the capacity of the mills will be doubled. An addition is now being put up at the east side of the main building and when completed another first-class paper machine will be put in. Probably also additional beating engines will be introduced as well as other facilities which will serve to double the capacity. When this project is carried out, this establishment will be one of the largest of the kind in the west. It enjoys advantages possessed by few paper mills and which enables it to do a prosperous business almost regardless of the condition of the market. We have dealt with this Company for a considerable time and can highly recommend it to the fraternity elsewhere, as well as to paper dealers, as being a very desirable concern with which to hold business relations. The product of the Appleton Paper Mills for the year 1878 aggregates to $200,000. Mr. H. J. Rogers is the Secretary and Treasurer of this Company and has entire charge of the business here.

RICHMOND BRO'S. PAPER MILL.

The past year has been a very prosperous one for this industry. It began the present year under very favorable conditions, numerous important enlargements and improvements having been made the previous year, by which its capacity was fully doubled. It was provided with a new and complete outfit of the best machinery and the character of the product this year has been, as might be expected, among the best to be found in the market. As evidence of this fact, it is quite worthy of remark that, notwithstanding the general depression in the paper industry, as well as otherwise, this mill has been kept busy, night and day, to fill its orders. Its products are exclusively wrapping paper of both straw and manilla grades. The books of Ricmond Bro's. show that their receipts during the year aggregate to $150,000. Of course, the success of this firm is largely due to the fact that it is composed of practical and experienced paper makers. They are conversant with the demands of the market and know how to meet them.

THE WESTERN WOOD PULP MILLS.

This is one of the most solid and successful of the numerous manufacturing establishments in this city. It is also one of the "pioneer" pulp mills in the country, having been built here seven years ago. During the succeeding time, with rare exceptions, the machinery has been constantly in motion, day and night. This has been necessary to meet the demands for the product by the various paper mills throughout the Western States. The pulp is utilized in the manufacture of print paper and is of a very superior quality. It is made wholly out of poplar wood—the latter being ground while green upon large and rapidly revolving stones designed for this purpose.

This concern has been of great benefit to the city and county. It furnishes employment to 30 hands and creates a demand for a kind of timber which in most places is, and in Appleton had hitherto, been worthless. Mr. O. W. Clark has had charge of these mills ever since they started, and the fact that their constant operation is attended with little or no friction is thus explained.

This establisnment is the property of Bradner, Smith & Co., of Chicago, one of the largest paper firms in the West, and is only one of the numerous and important enterprises in which they are engaged. They have several large mills at other points and do a heavy manufacturing business. The firm has a very extensive paper warehouse in Chicago and which is their central distributing point. They deal in all kinds of paper, from the coarsest to the finest grades, and have an immense trade throughout the Great West. We know of no better firm nor one that offers as many advantages to their patrons. They are courteous and obliging and are satisfied with small margins. After an experience in dealing with them of upwards of ten years, we can heartily and cheerfully commend the firm to the craft every-where, as well as to all other paper consummers. They are eminently deserveing of their success and prominence.

FLOURING MILLS.

Few, if any points in the whole country are better adapted to merchant milling than Appleton. Here we have an abundance of power and that of the right sort for enterprises of this kind. Then the country immediately surrounding and tributary to Appleton is one of the finest wheat growing sections of the Northwest. The grade of our wheat stands high in the best markets of the country, and indeed it is not surpassed by the similar products of any locality. The product of the contiguous territory is already quite extensive, but it will continue to increase every year as the development of the country proceeds. In addition to this our relations by rail and water with wheat growing sections in the interior and western portions of the State, as well as with Minnesota, Dakota and the country bordering upon the Mississippi, are such that unlimited supplies of this cereal can be had. Most of our mills are already provided with side tracks at their very doors and those hereafter to be established can have the same advantages. These considerations, together with the fact that the rates of transportation on lines reaching out into

the agricultural districts on one hand and to the leading markets of the country on the other, are as low in Appleton as are enjoyed by the manufacturers of any other interior town in the country.

THE APPLETON MILLS

Is one of the oldest establishments on our water, having been in continuous operation since 1852. Mr. Willy has been the proprietor for a number of years, and in this direction, as well as in other important undertakings, he has been eminently successful. But the Appleton Mills of to-day would scarcely be recognized as the original concern. The building itself has been frequently enlarged, its capacity many times increased and a great quantity of new and improved machinery has been added. Something has been done in this direction every season, and the past year, especially, Mr. Willy has expended a considerable sum in making improvements. A new set of crushers has been put in and the number of purifiers have also been increased. These mills are now thoroughly equipped, in every department, and are turning out a very superior grade of products, of which ample evidence is afforded by the ready sale with which they meet in the best markets of the country. Some idea of the magnitude of Mr. Willy's business will be had, when we state that his sales for the year 1878 will aggregate to $150,000. Of course the greater part of this immense product is shipped to eastern ports, but Mr. Willy also has a large local trade.

THE GENESEE MILLS.

This is one of the largest institutions of the kind in the State and there are but few in the West that have greater capacity. It is located in the Third Ward and is provided with one of the best water powers in the city. The building is a mammoth affair, being 75 feet square and five or six stories high. But large as it is, it is none too great to accommodate the vast system of machinery which is in operation. Not a year has passed, since Col. Conkey became the proprietor, but that he has made extensive and important improvements. Indeed it is enough to say, under this head, that he has kept steady pace with the progress which has been made in the milling industry of late years. Of course those who know anything about the matter, understand that it has been attended with immense strides. The evidence of it is seen in the superior brands of flour which are now used in nearly every household. Important improvements have also been made in the Genesee Mills, during the past season, considerable new machinery having been introduced. Col. Conkey has also expended a considerable amount, this year upon his fine water power—adding largely to the capacity thereof and to the permanence of the work by which it is maintained. The improvements made have involved an outlay of upwards of $3,000. The products of this establishment have a reputation in the leading flour markets at the East, which but few mills in the country enjoy. The Genesee Mills contain eight run of stone and the amount of its product for the year aggregates in value to $180,000.

THE OUTAGAMIE MILLS.

This is one of the oldest manufacturing establishments in the city. The present proprietors, however, did not engage in operating it until about two years ago. Since that time they have thoroughly overhauled it and have made some very important improvements. During the past year they have increased its capacity, to a considerable extent by putting in another run of stone—thus enabling them not only to do more work but to carry on their business to much better advantage. The mill is now in excellent working order and the character of its products will compare favora-

bly with the best. The proprietors, Messrs. Cross & Willy, are energetic and enterprising men and have devoted themselves with great industry to their business. The result is that they have already built up a fine business. They do a large amount of merchant work and in addition to this they have a large custom trade—their mill having a superior location for this purpose. The farmers are well pleased with the result of patronizing this establishment and the number is very large. The business of the firm, during the past year, shows a most gratifying increase—their receipts for the 12 months now closed aggregating to $40,000.

THE LAWRENCE MILLS.

This is now one of the leading establishments of the kind in Northern Wisconsin. In 1877 it was rebuilt, from bottom to top, and supplied with a large amount of new and improved machinery. Its capacity was also, at the same time, more than doubled. During the past season, two sets of large crushers have also been put in, besides considerable other machinery of a minor character. The Lawrence Mills are now as complete in every respect as experienced skill and money could make them. Notwithstanding the year '78 has been rather unfavorable for the milling industry, Messrs. Hauert & Weiland have done a large business—their sales for the year footing up to $158,000.

MAXWELL & BEARD'S MILL.

This establishment was erected on its present site, near the third lock, on the government canal, during the season of 1877. It has been operated to a considerable extent during the past year, but a great portion of the time has been spent in preparing more thoroughly for the better times which, it is hoped, the near future has in store. Another run of stone has been added this season and important improvements have otherwise been made. We expect to hear of the best reports from this concern by the close of another year.

BAUM & HUHN'S MILL.

The past season has witnessed the erection of this mill, on the lower water power. The work of putting in the machinery has been in progress for some time, and probably as soon as this number of the POST is in the hands of the reader, the establishment will be in complete operation. So far as the exterior is concerned, the mill is a modest looking affair; but we are assured that the machinery will be first-class and that its facilities in general will be such as to admit of first-class work being done. The proprietors are young men, but they are energetic and industrious, and we have no doubt that they will make their enterprise a fine success.

APPLETON FOUNDRY AND MACHINE SHOP.

The importance of having a first-class foundry and machine shop in our midst is something which our manufacturers have frequently had occasion to appreciate. Indeed it can meet their wants so perfectly and at short notice, that they could not well get along without it. It has facilities for doing a very wide range of work, from the turning out of the simplest casting to the manufacture of the heaviest kind of machinery.

During the past year, the firm lost one of its members—Mr. Ketchum having died several months ago. His place, however, has been supplied by Mr. Henry Bergman, a very skillful mechanic, to whom his interest has been leased. Mr. Morgan the other member of the firm, still abides with us and devotes his time and superior talents to the business. Some time since he invented a paper cutter which we desire to especially commend to printers. We have had one of his machines in use for upwards of a year and we take pleasure in stating that we have never used or seen anything of the kind which can compare with it in efficiency in performing the work for which it is designed. It is simple, easy to operate, never gets out of repair and can be relied upon for the most perfect work, at all times. A cut of this machine is shown elsewhere and printers will consult their interest by examining it carefully, and if they have need of a paper cutter, by ordering one at once. The POST, having learned its usefulness, could not keep house, without a Morgan cutter.

Notwithstanding the general depression in business, Ketchum & Morgan have done a prosperous business the past year—their receipts amounting to $25,000.

AGRICULTURAL IMPLEMENTS.

The success of the Appleton Manufacturing Company, during the few brief years of its existence, is somewhat remarkable. When they commenced they had most everything to contend against. In the first place their factory was not supplied with any permanent or reliable means of power, and to secure this required a new and important undertaking and one involving a considerable outlay. The energetic firm addressed themselves to the situation and in a short time, by the construction of several hundred feet of trunk, they secured a splendid power and of ample magnitude to answer their purpose. Again, in introducing their now famous seeder and other implements, they were met by wealthy concerns, prepared and determined to contest every inch of advancement by the new firm. But the magnitude of the latter's business to-day is the best of evidence as to how well they have succeeded. But their success was only accomplished by hard work, night and day. The members of the firm are all practical men and thoroughly understand the needs of the farmer in the way of machinery. Their best

PORTION OF THE LOWER WATER-POWER OF THE GREEN BAY AND MISSISSIPPI CANAL CO.

With Contemplated Improvements.

See page 23.

KUDERLING

TAKES THE LEAD.

He receives new goods every day; therefore
he can always show

The Most Attractive Stock,

AT THE VERY LOWEST PRICES.

Remember that I guarantee to save you
Five Per Cent. on your bill of dry
goods if you purchase of us.

Honest and Square Dealing Wins.

Quick Sales and Small Profits is our Motto.

COME IN AND SEE US.

L. H. KUDERLING.

energies were utilized in perfecting their seeder and in making it an indispensable implement to the thorough farmer. That they have succeeded, there is now no question among those competent to judge. It has surpassed all rivals in popular favor, and is to day the favorite machine where it is thoroughly known. Both as a seeder and cultivator, the Badger is complete and can be relied upon to do a great variety of work in a perfect manner. We refer the reader to a fine illustration of this machine elsewhere.

The Company also manufactures the peerless horse-hoe cultivator which has had such a large sale among the farmers, throughout the West, for several years past. It is adapted to a wide range of work and all who have used it find it quite indespensable to thorough farming. The Company manufactures various other implements which we have not space to notice and deals in farm machinery of all kinds. In fact, their establishment is headquarters, in Northern Wisconsin, for obtaining supplies of this description. We can commend the Company most heartily to retail dealers and to the farmers also, and with it business transactions will always be found profitable and satisfactory. The past year has been one of the most prosperous in their history—their sales having amounted to upwards of $65,000.

APPLETON STAVE FACTORY.

This is one of the pioneer manufacturing establishments of Appleton and there is probably none which has been of greater importance to the city and surrounding country. It has always furnished employment to a very large force of hands, all of whom receive cash for the work performed. The institution has also provided an excellent market for timber and its disbursements for this purpose, every winter, among the farmers of the adjacent towns, have proved of great advantage to them. The products

of the establishment consist entirely of flour barrel stock. The proprietors also have another factory at Kaukauna which is operated on an extensive scale. Their stock enjoys a splendid reputation, wherever it is known, and while they have a large local trade among our millers, the principal part of their sales is made elsewhere in Wisconsin and throughout other Western States.

Considerable improvements have been made in and about this factory the past season and it is now thoroughly equipped for the demands of a busy year.

Messrs G. W. Spaulding & Co., which is one of the very best firms on our river, inform us that their sales for '78 amount to $50,000 They have a regular force of 40 hands employed.

APPLETON CHAIR & BEDSTEAD FACTORY.

There is scarcely an establishment in this city which is of greater importance nor one which is doing more to spread our reputation abroad, as a manufacturing center, than the Appleton Chair and Bedstead Factory. Until a comparitively recent date the products of this institution consisted wholly of the more common articles of furniture, but latterly a new and very important departure has been made, viz : the manufacture of the very finest class of furniture, adapted to use in counting room, the private residence, the public hall and in fact every place where a superior article is required. To enable the company the better to carry out its plans, the services of a most skillful designer and worker in wood was employed, in the person of Mr. Thos. Hill. Other competent workmen were also engaged, specially adapted to certain departments and to perform the most excellent kind of work. New machinery was also introduced and other important improvements made to enable the company to fully carry out its designs. The experience of the company in introducing the products of this branch of their business has been most satisfactory. Numerous stores and society halls, here and eleswhere, have been supplied with most elaborate outfits of furniture, and it is not too much to say that in originality and elegance of design, as well as in the beauty and perfection of workmanship displayed, the work which this establishment has turned out is no where excelled. The Company is prepared to turn out the very best work in the line of walnut, oak and ash chamber suits, in the most popular designs, and secretaries, mantels, side-boards, etc. We can assure our readers who contemplate purchasing any of this class of articles that they can better be satisfied, with less money, at this factory than at any other establishment in the country.

Of course the manufacture of more ordinary furniture, including cane and wood-seat chairs, is continued by the company and on a large scale. It is needless to commend these goods for they are generally known throughout the West as being the best products of their class now manufactured. Retail dealers have found by experience that they can handle these goods with advantage and profit.

This company, of which Mr. Jas. F. Atkinson is the Secretary, Treasurer and business manager, employs a force of 80 hands and the receipts of its business for the year 1878 amount to $45,000.

PUMPS.

The Appleton Pump Factory is located on the Second ward water power and has been in operation since 1863. Mr. T. W. Brown is the proprietor and is one of our solid business men, financially and otherwise. He manufactures various styles and sizes of pumps and they are known to be among the very best in use. His factory is thoroughly equipped with machinery and his business is in

a prosperous condition. He has a large local trade and elsewhere, in Northwestern Wisconsin, as well. During the past year he has introduced some new machinery which adds considerably to his manufacturing facilities. Mr. Brown also deals quite extensively in lightning rods and handles the very best products of the market. His factory is located on the second Ward Water Power.

SASH, DOOR AND BLINDS.

The factory of which Messrs. Briggs & Beveridge are now the proprietors was established many years ago. Numerous important changes, however, have been made. The present spacious and substantial building was erected in the Spring of 1873 by Mr. Briggs. Somewhat later a partnership was formed between him and Mr. Wambold. During the season of 1877, the latter gentleman retired, disposing of his interest to Mr. Beveridge. During the same year numerous and important improvements were made which added largely to the facilities of the firm for doing business. Although trade has been generally depressed, during the year which has now just closed, this firm has had quite a prosperous trade. They have not only met all demands upon them but have shipped largely of their products to various other outside points. Their goods are very superior in quality and we can commend them heartily to retail dealers and dealers generally. The firm employ a force of 20 hands and do an annual business of $50,000.

BRICK, LIME, ETC.

J. H. MARSTON & CO.

This firm is successor to C. E. Fisher & Co., having bought out the old firm last month. They propose to continue in the manufacture of lime, at this point, and to handle building materials generally. The new company is now even better prepared than their predecessors to meet the public demands. They have put up another kiln this fall which will double the capacity of their works. The most skilled and experienced help that could be procured is in the employ of the new firm, and no pains or expense will be spared to meet all demands in a prompt and satisfactory manner. Marston & Co. will also deal in stone and mason's building materials in general. They have an excellent quarry at Clifton, the products of which are unsurpassed. It will be the aim of this firm to offer such inducements to the public as they cannot afford to overlook. And it will be for the advantage of all to patronize them when in need of anything in their line.

H. W. CARTER

has had a busy season at his brick yards, just outside of the city, on the banks of Lake Buttes Morts. He makes the best quality of brick ever used in this city. The are perfectly formed, have a uniform and regular surface and are very durable. Mr. Carter has had long experience in this line and is a skilled and practical brick-maker. The product of his yards, during the past season, amount to 700,-000 brick, most of which have been utilized in this locality.

TANNERIES.

PFEIFER & CO.

The tannery now owned by this firm is one of the oldest establishments on our water power. Not until August, 1877, however, did the present proprietors come into the possession of it. But since then it has been operated as it never had been before—to the full extent of its capacity and with an energy which characterizes an experienced and practical firm. During the past year and a half, while a very large business has been done, the proprietors have devoted a good share of their time to overhauling the establishment. So thorough has been their work, that there now remains

but liittle to be done. The tannery is now in excellent shape for doing business. The buildings have been largely repaired and a quantity of new and improved machinery has been put in by which the facilities have been improved and the capacity enlarged. Accordingly the business performed the past season is much greater than during any previous year of its history. The firm, Messrs. Pfeifer & Co., have a large leather house in Chicago, where the product of their Appleton factory is marketed.

KAMPS & FRIEUNDS TANNERY.

is located on the government canal, near the third lock. It is somewhat limited in its capacity, but is doing considerable work, notwithstanding. It is very well provided with machinery and other facilities for manufacturing and the quality of its products commands for them a ready market.

IRON-MAKING.

THE APPLETON FURNACE.

The fact that the iron furnace in this city is one of the few out of the whole number in the United States now in operation, is good evidence (1,) that the establishment is being well managed and (2) that this point has advantages which few others enjoy. The cost of power is a mere nothing and the fact that the enormous freights are taken and delivered at the very yards of the establishment is a consideration involving great economy. Indeed these are probably the secrets which enable it to operate while others are obliged to close. This furnace turns out the very best grade of charcoal pig iron, and when there is any demand at all, it meets with a ready sale.

The Company has a large force of hands in its constant employ and the receipts of its business for the year 1878 will amount to $120,000.

H. D. Smith, an experienced iron manufacturer, is the Secretary and Treasurer of the Company.

LUMBER.

During the early part of the past year, Messrs. Whorton Bro's, one of our heaviest lumber firms, having become largely interested elsewhere, disposed of the site on which their saw mill was located and it is now occupied by a more important enterprise. They also sold out their stock on hand, with their good will, etc. to

MESSRS. RAMSAY & JONES,

a firm of enterprising young men, who are now supplying and will hereafter meet all demands for lumber, in this locality, which amounts to a very extensive trade. They have most excellent facilities for this purpose. They have a large tract of land in the "Menomonee district," covered with the very best of pine. They also have mills of great capacity, so situated that they can be reached from this place by both rail and water, and the products of which can be delivered here at the least possible expense. Their yards are located on the flat, just south of Grand Chute Island, and between the railroad and the government canal. They have been very busy the past season putting in a stock of lumber so extensive as to be fully up to the demands of the city and surrounding country. They engaged in business here last June and since then they have had a very handsome trade. The demands upon them are growing and will no doubt continue to increase. They carry a stock which enables them to fill any order, and the people appreciate the fact that their facilities are such as to enable them to undersell dealers less favorably circumstanced.

ROSE & HEATH.

This is one of the old, as it is also one of the solid firms, engaged in manufacturing on the river. They have always commanded a liberal share of the local trade and have also exported largely to other points. Their mill is located on the lower water power. The past year, however, has been a most unfavorable one for them, and they have done but a limited business, compared to that of previous years. On account of the entire absence of snow last winter, they were unable to get in any stock, and the consequence was that their operations were very much abridged. However, with a favorable winter, this year, they will doubtless do a large business the coming season. They manufacture hard and soft lumber, a variety of wagon stock and broom handles.

HUBS AND SPOKES.

There is no better place for the manufacture of wagon stock, on a large scale than Appleton. The forests immediately surrounding abound in the very best grade of timber, and the experience of our manufacturers during the past season also demonstrates the fact that, by means of accessible railway lines and water courses, a large section of country can be drawn upon, at any time, for the necessary supplies. Moreover the advantage of cheap transportation, for manufactured stock, as well as raw material, here obtains, and of course the best of water power privileges can be had.

THE APPLETON HUB AND SPOKE FACTORY.

This is one of the oldest industries of the kind in this part of the state and it has also been one of the most successful. But it has never had a more prosperous year than the past one has proved to be; and this, too, notwithstanding the indications at the beginning of the season were anything but encouraging. It is true that the market promised fairly but the winter of '77-'78 was most unfavorable for securing a stock of timber. The entire season brought not a single day of sleighing, and to the ordinary observer the prospect appeared most gloomy. However, Messrs. Marston & Beveridge did not propose to succumb to circumstances. Accordingly, instead of depending wholly upon the home supply, they arranged for stock at various outside points, touching the rail and water lines of transportation, reaching out from this city. The result was that they secured a splendid stock of timber—fully equal to any which they had ever purchased at their factory, and at no greater cost. Having settled this point in their favor, a vigorous season of manufacturing at once began. Orders commenced to come in thick and fast and every part of their facilities had to be brought into requisition to meet these orders. And [the demand upon them was no spasmodic affair. The year has continued to the close as it opened and their establishment has been kept busy the entire year to meet the requirements of the market upon them. And notwithstanding their stock was much larger than common, it was all utilized earlier than usual. Although the success of the year may be accounted for, to some extent, upon the improvement of the market, in their line, yet this does not wholly explain the facts. The products of this establisment have an enviable reputation among the wagon manufactures of the west and if there is any demand at all, this firm is among the few who can take advantage of the opportunity. They make it a point to buy nothing but the very best of stock and their facilities for manufacturing are such as to enable them to show the best results obtainable. The sales of this firm, during the past year amount to a very gratifying increase over those of the previous year—footing up, as they do, to $55,000. Marston & Beveridge contemplate material enlargements another year which will add considerably to their capacity.

BILLINGS & MORRISON'S FACTORY.

During the year which is now closed, this has been one of the busiest establishments on the whole river. Anticipating a a liberal demand for their prod-

ucts early in the year, this firm, on account of the unfavorableness of the previous winter, abandoned all hopes of securing their yearly stock from the immediate locality, and made ample arrangements for an adequate supply of timber at various outside points. And their sagacity has proved of great advantage to them. Indeed they have never before witnessed so prosperous a year as the past hâs proved to be. As the most gratifying evidence of this fact that can be introduced, we may state that their product of the previous year has more than thribbled. They had the advantage of beginning the year, with a most excellent reputation for their products throughout the west, and the result has been that they could not possibly fill the orders which crowded in upon them from time to time. Their receipts for the year aggregate to $25,000. This, as against $8,000 for 1877, is surely as flattering an exhibit as could be expected. The prospects of the firm for the coming year are also very encouraging.

GEO. KREISS' HUB AND SPOKE EACTORY is located on the government canal and is one of the oldest institutions of the kind in this part of the State. Its products consist of wagon stock in general, including hubs, spokes, fellœs, etc. The best of material is used to supply the factory and as the process of making is thoroughly performed, the product finds ready sale in the best markets throughout the West. In common with others in his line, the past year has proved a very prosperous one to Mr. Kreiss.

GENERAL MACHINE WORK.

During the past year, Hart & Page have put up a small factory and equipped it with suitable facilities for making all kinds of repairs and doing general machine work. A satisfactory success has attended their efforts, thus far, and we have no doubt the firm will continue to prosper in the future.

APPLETON WOOLEN MILLS.

This has proved one of the most indispensible, as it has been one of the most prosperous establishments, on the line of Fox River. To the farmer in this community and neighboring counties as well has it been of great value, and with whom it has always sustained intimate relations. It receives his wool product at the highest cash price and furnishes him with goods, adapted to his uses, upon which he can rely as being superior in every respect. The city also has occasion to appreciate its great importance. It furnishes employment to 118 operatives and disburses in wages every year upwards of $17,000. At these times, when the supply of all kinds of labor exceeds the demand to such an extent, the benefit of an industry of this kind to the community which immediately surrounds it, can hardly be overestimated.

It is a most gratifying fact that, notwithstanding the general depression which prevails in business, and the specially unfavorable time for the manufacture of woolen fabrics, the Appleton Mills have seen but few idle days during any of the recent years. Of course there is an adequate cause for this surprising activity. First, the superior business management of the concern has a great deal to do with its success. It is wholly in the hands of young men, but during their brief career, they have shown remarkable enterprise, tempered with prudence and foresight which is a rare business virtue, even among men who are their seniors by many years. These young men have applied themselves to business with faithfulness and determination, and the result is that their efforts have been crowned with a fine success. Their policy radically differs from that of most manufacturers in their line in the West. Rather than to depend upon retail dealers for their patronage, which is somewhat precarious at best and is attended with more or less losses, this firm has disposed of its entire product to the leading jobbers in Chicago, Detroit, Cleveland, Toledo, Milwaukee, St. Paul and Minneapolis. Of course their profits on a given amount of goods are much less on this account, but in the end they are the gainers, as there is but little or any losses to be charged up at the end of the year. Of course this arrangement with wholesale dealers could not obtain, unless the products of this factory were first-class in every respect. But that such is the case is evident from the fact that the jobbers who once secure their handling are always anxious to continue the arrangement. Indeed, woolen fabrics which present the brand "standard" have the most ready passport to popular favor.

The products of the Appleton Woolen Mills consist of all woolen flannels, knitting yarns, balmorals, clouded, fancy colors and plain.

The books of Hutchinson & Co. show that they have consumed 200,000 pounds of wool during the year 1878 and that their receipts for this period foot up to $125,000. We feel like specially congratulating this firm on the success of the past year.

DICKERSON SHUTTER WORKS.

This is a new industry in Appleton, the works having been constructed, during the past year. The product consists of a new kind of fixtures for outside window blinds and which are certain to have a widespread sale when their merits become known. The utility of the fixtures consist of affording to the occupant of a room perfect control of outside blinds, without raising the window. The blinds can be either wholly or partially opened or closed, and locked securely at any point. The slats can also be adjusted so as to admit of any volume of light desired or it can be excluded entirely by closing them, all of which can be done by simple movements of the interior attachment. The resulting benefits are many and need not here ·be enumerated. We feel certain that this device will meet a want long felt and that, ere long, it will become immensely popular throughout the country. We take pleasure in calling attention to the announcement of the Company elsewhere, which is also accompanied with an illustration explaining, to some extent, the invention of which we have spoken.

HORSE NAIL WORKS.

The enterprise of manufacturing horse nails was started in this city, about one year ago. While a very considerable amount of manufacturing has been done during the intervening period, a good deal of time, as might be expected, has been employed in laying the ground work for extensive and permanent operations. We are very much pleased to be able to inform our readers that the enterprise is now thoroughly established and in operation to the full extent of its capacity. Indeed we may say that this has been the case since August last, at which time the work of putting ·in new and improved machinery was completed. The Company, here engaged. manufactures one of the very best nails in the market. If evidence of this statement is wanted, we may submit the fact that it meets with ready and rapid sale wherever introduced. This is an unusual thing with the products of any new establishment, and especially with horse nails. · The consumers of these goods are unusually prejudiced in favor of some well known article, having an established reputation ; but a few months have sufficed for the Champion nail to force its way into conspicuous and popular favor. Indeed the works have been running night and day for the two or three months past, and at the present time are

at least four weeks behind in filling their orders. On account of this most gratifying demand for their products, the Company will double the capacity of the works about the 10th of January, 1879, and are now making arrangements accordingly. The unmistakable evidences now are that this industry will soon develop into one of the most important in this valley. This company is composed of thorough, experienced, and practical business men. The officers thereof are as follows :

President—S. M. Dorr, Rutland, Vt.
Sec'y and Treasurer—Wm. H. Steele, Appleton, Wis. ·
Superintendent—E. F. Decker, Appleton, Wis.
General Agent—Wm. R. Dorr, Appleton, Wis.

FANNING MILLS, ETC.

John Clapper does a snug business in the manufacture of fanning mills and milk safes, both of which articles are highly thought of. His factory is located north of the depot, in the fifth ward.

RECAPITULATION.

To present in a succinct form, and as a matter in which we know very many of our readers will be interested, the business transacted by the Appleton manufacturers during the year of 1878, we herewith submit a recapitulation of the facts and figures above presented in detail. As will be seen the result shows a most gratifying increase over the exhibit which we were able to make, in our last Annual Review. This fact speaks louder than words of the steady progress which Appleton is making towards a distinction as a manufacturing center which few cities can hope to rival.

	No. hands employed.	Product for the year
Farming Implements,	20	65,000.
Furniture,	80	45,000.
Flour,	43	548,000.
Hubs and spokes,	45	75,000.
Iron,	35	120,000.
Lumber,	17	63,000.
Leather,	22	31,000.
Lime Brick, etc..	10	15,000.
Machinery	15	25,000.
Pumps,	3	8,000.
Paper (Print & Wrap)	185	410,000.
Staves and Heading,	45	50,000.
Sash, Doors and Blinds.	20	50,000.
Woolen Goods,	118	125,000.
Wood Pulp.	65	150,000.
Others.	30	55,000.
Total,	743	$1,835,000

THE APPLETON POST.

ANNUAL REVIEW.

1879.

ACKNOWLEDGEMENTS.

It is proper that our acknowledgments should accompany this issue of the POST to our manufacturers, merchants and business men generally for the substantial encouragement which we have received at their hands. Indeed, it is only by their hearty co-operation that we have been enabled to make the POST what we believe it is to-day, viz., the most complete work of the kind ever undertaken by any country newspaper in behalf of the locality in which it is published. We, therefore, feel grateful to all persons upon whom we have drawn for favors and information, the result of which is presented upon these numerous pages.

Our special thanks are also due to Mrs. Stansbury, for her charming and appropriate contribution contained on the opposite page; and to W. J. Allen, Esq., and Prof. Hyde who have rendered us very important aid in the preparation of this work. We have likewise drawn heavily upon our efficient City Clerk, P. J. Cirkel, for the facts and figures presented under the "municipal" head, and upon Prof. Schmidt, Dr. Randall and Edward West for other favors. Finally, to one and all to whom we are indebted, we would express our cordial thanks for numerous favors and courtesies received.

OUR ANNUAL REVIEW.

This is the fourth occasion, on which the POST greets its numerous readers, in the city, county and elsewhere with its Annual Review. We shall not attempt to conceal the pride with which we present this number, for that would be a spurious and absurd modesty. But we trust this feeling is not peculiar to ourselves. Indeed, we have faith to believe that our readers and the people generally will peruse these pages with a gratification somewhat akin to that which we have experienced in their preparation. Our patrons certainly have more interest in the contents than we have any right to assume. It is devoted, in a general way, to the making known of the great resources and advantages of Appleton, in which their material interests and prospects are embraced. A considerable portion of the space is also occupied in the reviewing of individual enterprises, in which the people whom the POST aims to serve, are directly concerned. In short, it has been our ambition to leave no subject untouched which would naturally come within the scope of an undertaking of this kind, and we have endeavored to make this number such as will be received with interest at home and as can be distributed, with good results, abroad.

In collecting the facts and figures which form the basis of the work displayed on these pages, the utmost care has been exercised, and if for no other reason, we must be permitted to commend the conclusions reached as being significant for their reliability. The importance of this feature, both for home and foreign consumption, cannot be overestimated, and this point we have kept steadily in mind.

We have faith to believe that the work and progress of the year, detailed and summarized in these columns, in a manner easy to comprehend, will be a source of extreme satisfaction to every resident or friend of the city or county. That our prosperity and development are thus indicated, no person who will examine the evidence can deny. Indeed, as herein appears, the magnitude to which our material interests have attained, is a subject upon which our people may well exchange hearty congratulations; and that it will attract some attention throughout the country, is a result reasonably to be expected. It is proper to suggest here, and worth while to bear in mind, that the result achieved is not in consequence of general activity but rather the fruit of enterprise and advantages peculiar to this locality.

That the custom inaugurated by the POST, a few years ago, of annually reviewing the progress, events and business of the past year is attended with wholesome results is a proposition which, we are assured, has the cordial assent of our readers in particular and the general public as well. That the form in which this work is, this week, presented will be specially acceptable, we have no doubt whatever. It meets the convenience of the reader, as a cumbersome sheet could not; and, as it is more easily preserved, the resulting benefits are likely to be more permanent than could be secured in the newspaper form. It is our intention to continue this method hereafter, so that, when three or more are issued, they can be bound in one volume, by those who may desire, for permanent reference in the future.

And now, with this brief introduction, we submit our Fourth Annual Review to our readers—leaving it with them to criticise its defects and, if it appears worthy, to approve of its merits. But, whatever be the tendency of their comments, we wish one and all "A Happy New Year."

OLD AND NEW.

JANUARY 1st, 1879

Out-worn at last, with all his race the old year goes to rest ;
His hands are folded wearily across his gallant breast.
No friend could wish him back again, of all who loved him best.

He heard the storm of battle rave beyond that storied main,
Whose calm tides beat the shore that owned the haughty Caesar's reign ;
And saw, along the Eastern sky, the fiery Crescent wane.

Yet not from Plevna's fortress walls, where cannon-thunders beat ;
And not from pass or dim defile, where Turk and Northmen met ;
Nor crimson field where, heart to heart, their bayonets were set ;—

Nor yet from bloodless strife of courts, where hostile powers arrayed
Of subtle wit and eloquence, unsheathed the glittering blade,
And turn of phrase or stroke of pen, an empire marred or made ;

But where, above our native land death's shadow settled down,
And wave on wave of anguish rolled from smitten town to town,
He called his peerless heroes forth to wear a martyr-crown—

Oh ! on the field where Freedom's flag is waving proud and high,
And thunder-peals of victory rend all the lurid sky,
With fame's elixir at the lip, men may not fear to die !

But these, with kiss of wife and child yet clinging warm and sweet,
From happy doors of Northern homes, went forth with steady feet
To face the fever-death that walked, unstayed, the Southern street.

Fearless they breathed the tainted air from poison fountains fed,
And saw, like Moloch carved in bronze, the sun glare hot and red
Above the dying side by side with yet unburied dead.

Through midnight-watches dread and deep, in many a noisome room,
They grappled with the spectral hands that clutched them in the gloom
Unbroken by one dawning ray across the skies of doom.

The hands that spared not brother's blood, at Liberty's behest,
Grew tender as a mother's now, above her darling's rest,
Till hearts, the sword could ne'er compel, love's mastery confest.

Ah! dearer than to pilgrim feet is holy Mecca's shrine,
Shall be the graves of those who fell in service so divine!
Their children's children's lips shall boast a more than royal line!

So, from the foulest reeks of death, hope's snowy lilies grew;
And love, though late, the pearl of peace from deeps of suffering drew;
And on the ruined Old arose the temple of the New!

Why does the New Year come in winter time,
And wrapped in mantle white of fleecy snow?
His greeting song alone the stormy rhyme
Of gales that through the leafless branches blow?

Can streamlets sing when all the flowers are dead?
Or skies be glad whence birds have flown away?
The sunbeam for the rose be comforted?
Or lonely hearts keep winter holiday?

Ah! my heart, with all thy learning, art thou still so slow discerning
Joy of hope than joy of having more complete?
Better first are tears than laughter, for the comfort waiting after,
And the song that ends the sighing is more sweet!

So the New Year in his bosom hides all spring-time, bud and blossom,—
Summer lights asleep on land and sea,—
Autum's misty, purple splendor,—moons of harvest large and tender,
Climbing slowly up the skies to be.

All the birds shall pipe before him, and a cloudless heaven shine o'er him,
And the earth be strewn with blossoms in his way,—
All the little brooks run swifter, and the crested laurel lift her
Purple banners to the glad, triumphal day!

Many a grave the brown leaves cover, will the New Year sprinkle over
With hope's tender garlands white as snow;
For the bitter herbs of sorrow, in the sunshine of to-morrow
We may smile to see love's perfect roses blow!

And when, at length, adown life's sunset sky,
Its cares and hopes may fade, and Memory shine,
A lonely star, with tender, mournful eye,—
Still point us gently, O, thou Hand divine!

Beyond the world where all our years grow old,
And gathering mists obscure the crystal sphere,
To where the jasper walls and streets of gold
Reflect the light of Heaven's eternal year!

—MARY A. P. STANSBURY.

RAILROADS.

THE GREAT HIGHWAYS FOR TRAVEL AND TRANSPORTATION—APPLETON IS LIBERALLY PRO-
VIDED WITH FACILITIES OF THIS KIND—TWO IMPORTANT AND COMPETING LINES NOW
IN OPERATION—CONNECTING US WITH COMMERCIAL CENTERS ON ONE HAND AND A
PRODUCTIVE TERRITORY UPON THE OTHER—WHAT HAS BEEN ACCOMPLISHED THE
PAST YEAR AND WHAT IS CONTEMPLATED FOR THE FUTURE—FIGURES SHOWING A DE-
TAILED REPORT OF THE BUSINESS FOR THE YEAR.

The rapid development of the Western Continent which has been the wonder of the world has been owing to the construction of railroads and the facilities which they have provided more than to any other agency. It is true that the building of these thoroughfares has been a great tax upon the people, both in their capacity as a nation and as muncipalities. Immense subsidies have been granted and secured and in divers other ways have the people shared in the great outlays which have been made for this purpose. Moreover the rights acquired at what would seem, in one sense, to be at the sacrifice of the public interests, have often been grossly abused by the corporations obtaining them. But with all of the iniquities practiced and evils that have resulted, few men live to-day who will deny that, with the debits and credits properly entered, the country has been immensely the gainer from our vast system of railways which unite the country with bands of iron and steele. They are the avenues upon which the agents of commerce may hurry to and fro, and the products of human industry find swift and ready transit. They are adapted to all climes and are quite independent of the elements. The extreme heat of the tropics cannot create an agent to endanger their operations and the rigor of northern zones can, at most, only a trifle restrict their usefulnesss. There is no distance so great which they cannot overcome, and there is no country where they are not required which has resources to be developed. In a word, railroads are the most potent material agents which civilization has in her employ, and they never weary in obeying her behests. They respond to every call, and bear burdens with faithfulness and precision.

Appleton is fortunate first in having been provided with ample facilities for travel and transportation by land to meet her wants now and hereafter; and secondly, in having escaped the extortions of which many interior towns have had occasion to complain.

THE CHICAGO AND NORTHWESTERN RAILROAD.

This is one of the most important thoroughfares in the whole country, and the importance to Appleton of being situated on its route is very great. The ramifications of this road are so great that there is hardly an important section of the country which it does not touch. It also places us in connection with other important lines which reach out in every direction through the country. Thus are placed within our reach the means of obtaining our supply of crude materials from a source which is inexhaustible and of seeking a market for our manufactured products at as little tax upon our industries as could be expected in the most highly favored locality.

This road has seven distinct divisions which reaches into as many states and describing an aggregate distance of over 2,000 miles. The facilities of the road are not surpassed by those of any other corporation in the country. Every mile of the track is in excellent condition and it is the policy of the company to keep their property in the best of repair. Within the past few years the old tracks of iron have been removed and more substantial paths of steel have taken their place. The rolling stock of the company is immense in extent. Freight cars by the thousands, adapted to all kinds of traffic, have been provided to accommodate their immense business at various points. The traveling coaches are as fine as can be seen anywhere and the appliances of the road are otherwise first class and of a character to best supply the wants and comforts of its patrons. The management is little short of perfect. An accident on this line, resulting from recklessness or indifference, is unknown, and even the possibility of such a disaster is not tolerated. So far as Appleton's relations with this company are concerned few of our people have ever had occasion to believe that it has no soul. Indeed it is an honorable competitor for our business and is courteous and liberal to an unusual degree. As will be seen, it performs a large carrying business for this city. Mr. C. B. Morrison, the agent of the company, has furnished us with the figures which enables us to present a report of the business, at this point, in detail. It is as follows by months :

FREIGHT RECEIVED.

	Pounds.	Charges.
January,	1,922,300	$ 1,959.17
February,	1,671,312	1,890.59
March,	1,197,065	1,842.30
April,	2,865,606	3,319.08
May,	2,536,214	2,937.79
June,	2,909,650	3,475.30
July,	2,024,714	2,540.34
August,	3,594,978	4,068.53
September,	3,609,266	4,254.79
October,	5,292,059	5,179.46
November,	4,325,189	4,288.61
December,	4,000,000	4,000.00
Total	35,948,353	40,295.96

FREIGHT FORWARDED.

	Pounds.	Charges.
January,	1,494,730	2,296.21
February,	2,421,630	3,385.42
March,	1,146,150	1,647.41
April,	2,253,975	2,936.69
May,	2,088,005	2,983.92
June,	1,900,380	2,545.93
July,	2,626,850	2,784.05
August,	1,780,030	2,388.22
September,	1,999,940	2,609.15
October,	1,994,130	2,889.61
November,	2,074,490	2,679.74
December,	1,900,000	
Total	23,677,310	29,154.25

TICKET SALES.

During the year, 13,500 persons have bought tickets, at the station in this city and have paid the company therefor $25,337.61.

MILWAUKEE LAKE SHORE AND WESTERN RAILWAY.

As in the case of the Chicago and Northwestern, the building of this road upon the route which it describes, involved a considerable outlay to the people of Appleton—aid having been voted to both enterprises. But few can be found to-day who comprehend the real interests of the city who regret these investments. Especially in the latter case have the benefits secured been of the utmost importance to this locality. The road accommodates the wants of our manufacturing interests as they had never been provided for before, and in

such a way as to result in a great saving. The line of the road is directly through the center of the manufacturing part of the city and is very convenient of access from every direction. And the plans of the company is to ultimately reach every establishment on the river by building spurs or side tracks, connecting with the main line. Already considerable progress has been made in this direction. Several thousand feet of track has been built this season and another year a large amount of similar work will be done. The economy of the arrangement by which a manufacturer can receive raw materials from the cars at his very door and ship his products from the same point is apparent. The saving aggregates to a large amount during the year and would make quite a handsome profit in itself.

The general route described by this road is of great importance to this city. It gives us a swift and direct connection with a fine Lake port, only 40 miles distant and places us in intimate communication with Milwaukee, the metropolis of the state—thus also affording us a competing line with the Northwestern.

The extention of this road westward to New London, which was accomplished in 1876, has been of great consequence to this city. It secured us a connection, at that point, with the G. B. & M. R. R., running thence west to the Mississippi and into Minnesota. It has therefore rendered this splendid region of country directly tributary to this locality and upon which we can draw for a great variety of supplies in the shape of agricultural and other products, which our industries require in abundance.

During the past season this road has been extended westward 20 miles, upon a new route and through a very productive country.

Its farther limit is now Clintonville, a flourishing village in Waupaca County. It is the intention of the Company to continue the extention of the road from that point northward, to some point on Lake Superior. When this is accomplished, which will be at an early day, a vast section of country, rich in timber and mineral resources will be rendered tributary to Appleton and upon which we may depend for supplies for decades to come.

During the past year, as well as the year previous, this road has done a very large business in this city. Mr. G. L.

Young, the agent, has furnished us with the following figures which explains the details:

FREIGHT RECEIVED.

Months.	Pounds.	Charges.
January	3,638,800	$ 1,080.15
February	2,529,390	1,000.61
March	2,550,510	1,105.69
April	4,194,120	1,147.57
May	3,792,130	1,011.12
June	4,143,590	1,098.40
July	2,838,890	751.33
August	3,736,480	850.66
September	3,979,148	939.41
October	4,220,819	1,698.40
November	3,960,851	1,412.52
December	4,000,000	1,670.00
Total	46,584,723	13,800.53

FREIGHT FORWARDED.

Months.	Pounds.	Charges.
January	2,140,600	1,843.24
February	2,441,330	1,310.40
March	1,720,700	1,586.59
April	2,429,690	1,773.40
May	2,589,750	1,811.37
June	2,047,270	1,351.64
July	2,031,230	1,291.88
August	2,182,300	1,382.50
September	2,210,740	1,447.83
October	2,894,070	2,524.30
November	3,100,980	2,422.09
December	3,000,000	2,300.00
Total	28,784,670	21,297.36

The ticket sales of this road for the year, amount to $5.179.33.

OTHER RAILWAY PROSPECTS.

During the fall months of the year, now closed, the Wis. C. R. R. Co. has had surveys made from Menasha to this city, with the view of extending their line to this point. Appleton has become a place of much importance and the extent of its business has become so much of an attraction to all railroads in this vicinity that self interest prompts them to establish relations with this point. The Wisconsin Central Company will undoubtedly undertake the project mentioned, another year, at the latest, and the Milwaukee and St. Paul Co. will probably soon follow suit.

OUR COMMERCIAL ENTERPRISES.

THE RECORD OF THE YEAR '78 QUITE GRATIFYING, SO FAR AS THEY ARE CONCERNED —THE FIGURES INDICATING A CONSIDERABLE INCREASE OVER THE SALES OF THE PREVIOUS YEAR —THE TOTAL TRADE OF THE CITY AMOUNTING TO THE HANDSOME AGGREGATE OF $1,770,200 —THE RESULT PRESENTED BEING BASED UPON THE FACTS OBTAINED FROM PERSONAL VISITS TO EVERY PLACE OF BUSINESS, HIGH AND LOW— THE WHOLE ACCOMPANIED BY APPROPRIATE OBSERVATIONS AND COMMENTS.

PREFATORY.

There is no division of our work, on such an occasion as the present, that we approach with greater interest than that which is now before us. The mercantile trade of a city is of the greatest importance and to the student of our business life and progress an examination of the subject cannot otherwise than be attended with interesting revelations. Especially have our recent visits to the various establishments in the city been most agreeable and interesting. To converse with the merchant upon the successes of the year, the prospects and probabilities of the future, to congratulate him upon his prosperity and to sympathize with him as to his tribulations is not a distasteful duty to the journalist. It serves to establish and preserve friendly relations and places the observing chronicler of local events in possession of important information which he can, if he will, utilize for the public good.

1878.

In the further introduction of this subject, it affords us great pleasure to state, as the result of careful investigation and the facts thus gleaned, that a measurable degree of prosperity has attended our dealers during the past year. Many of them have increased their sales, while but few have suffered from any diminution, in this respect, and the general result is that the aggregate trade of the city reaches a considerably larger amount than it did the year last preceding. All the firms now engaged in business are pretty firmly established, financially and otherwise, and will weather the gale of hard times as successfully as any similar class of business men elsewhere in the country.

THE FIELD FULLY OCCUPIED.

It is the aim of the POST to attract attention to Appleton. That is doubtless apparent upon these pages and we shall not here attempt to conceal it. But it is no part of our purpose to misreprothe situation. We may, therefore, frankly state, in justice to those who may be looking in this direction, as well as to those now engaged here, that, so far as mercantile establishments are concerned, the city is abundantly supplied. This is not only true in a general way but in each particular line as well. We have all that present demands warrant, and even if our future progress is as rapid as we now anticipate, several years must elapse befor the number of our retail dealers can be successfully increased. There is plenty of room here for men of enterprise and capital to engage themselves profitably, but not as venders of merchandise of any kind. The opportunities and advantages for manufacturing are unlimited and the number or kind of industries cannot be multiplied to such an extent as to interfere with the prosperity of one or many. We are persuaded to indulge in these remarks out of regard for the truth, a consideration of the real interests of the city and to the end that no undertaking will be encouraged that would be likely to prove a failure.

THE WORK IN HAND.

As the reader proceeds, he will notice that, in reviewing the mercantile transactions of the city, we have continued the policy adopted last year, viz.: omitting the figures in connection with each firm, showing the amount of business which it has done during the year. This plan we have found to be generally satisfactory and it also promotes the accuracy of our work. We have obtained the figures, however, and have made use of them in the final summing up and in that the public is most interested.

DRY GOODS.

This department, in Appleton especially, constitutes the leading feature of mercantile trade. And the city has ample occasion to be proud of the numerous fine establishments engaged in this line. We particularize as follows:

PETTIBONE & CO.

This is essentially a pioneer firm in Appleton, having been established here upwards of 18 years; but it has not been contented with the primitive method of doing business. It has not only kept pace with the growth of Appleton, but it has rather been in the advance. The policy of the firm has always been, and now more than ever, to present to the public as fine attractions as can be found in the State. They carry an immense stock, including a comprehensive assortment of the various grades of goods in their line. In the matter of fine goods especially, Pettibone's is headquarters. Pettibone & Co. buy for cash and share the resulting benefits with their customers in the way of small margins. The rapid increase of the business of this firm has necessitated the material enlargement of their store which has been accomplished, at an expense of $2,000, during the past year. In the new part, which has been finely fitted up and furnished, is a well regulated and skillfully conducted millinery department, which has become a leading feature of the firm's business. The management of this establishment is in the hands of Mr. Geo. Peabody, and to his sagacity, tact and enterprise may a large measure of its success be ascribed. Indeed he may be said to be master of the situation. We are glad to be able to state that the sales of Pettibone & Co., during the past year, have been much greater than ever before.

CLARK & EDWARDS

is another of our leading firms in the dry goods line who are deserving of the fine success which they have achieved. They have one of the most attractive stores in the city and enjoy a very large patronage from both town and country. They also do a considerable wholesale trade. Notwithstanding the increased competition, the sales of this firm for '78 are fully 20 per cent. larger than during any previous year. They carry a very large and superior line of goods and otherwise offer such inducements as secures for them numerous customers from adjacent towns as well as from this immediate locality.

FLEMING'S TRADE PALACE.

Early in the season, the firm of A. D. Fleming & Co. contracted with J. A. Bertschy for the rebuilding of the block, destroyed by fire, one year age. This was accomplished early in August, shortly after which, the firm mentioned occupied the building with a mammoth stock of dry goods. This building, as will be seen by the illustration elsewhere, is one of the finest for the purpose, in the whole State. The first floor is double the size of an ordinary store but all available space is nevertheless occupied with goods. The success of the firm, thus far, is very gratifying and of course their trade will continue to increase. One great secret of their success is that they do business strictly on a cash basis. They are therefore prepared to offer better inducements to customers than could otherwise be afforded. Their enterprise, on such a scale, was at first considered and experiment but that point is now passed and it may be reckoned as one of the permanent institutions of the place.

L. H. KUDERLING

succeeded the firm of Kuderling & Schwantes, early in the year. He is one of the most thorough young merchants in the city and his success has been marked and gratifying. He understands the wants of the trade thoroughly and devotes himself with energy to supplying them. He receives his full proportion of the best class of trade in the city and county. His stock of goods is extensive, his assortment always complete—two considerations having great weight with the purchaser. Mr. Kuderling's sales for '78 exceed those of the previous year by a considerable sum.

GROCERIES.

No branch of business in Appleton is conducted on a more extensive or creditable scale than this. We have numerous fine establishments, as well as divers smaller ones, all of whom report a successful year.

D. B. BAILEY

succeeded the firm of Bailey & Ballard, late in the year. He is one of the best known dealers in the city and those now engaged in trade here who ante-date him are very few. His success is conspicuous as it is deserved. It is not the re-

sult of chance. Probably no dealer in the city has striven so hard, early and late, to accomplish this end. But diligence has not been the only agency in his employ. Mr. Bailey has superior business qualifications; he is prompt, careful and courteous. He provides the public with as superior a line of goods as the best market affords, and as he does business on a cash basis, his customers have the benefit of low prices. Besides doing a leading grocery trade, Mr. Bailey makes a specialty of handling hardware and in which line he has an extensive trade also. His receipts for '78 are probably as large as those of any house in Appleton.

PATTON BRO'S,

a firm composed of energetic young men, occupy a leading position in the city ar grocers. Indeed, this is one of the most complete establishments of the kind in this part of the State. They have earned the reputation of being excellent caterers to the public taste. They not only deal in the more staple articles, in their line, but make a specialty of all sorts of delicacies, including the finest of fruits and choice table supplies in general. The past year has been one of the most prosperous in this firm's history. The Patton Bros. also conduct a branch house in the First Ward, established last summer. The enterprise has proved a fine success.

SPAULDING & PRATT

have now been engaged in business about two years, but this time has enabled the firm to establish itself permanently in the grocery trade. They carry a superior line of goods and one that is selected with evident skill and care. The firm commands a very liberal share of the trade of the city and their sales for the year compare well with the receipts of leading establishments.

THE PARDEE BRO'S

commenced business on the 14th of October, last and at once dropped into a very fine trade. They are energetic young men and had the advantage of possessing an extended and very desirable acquaintance. Their stock is fresh and new and they neglect no effort to make it an object for the people to deal with them. The extent of their sales, thus far, is highly satisfactory.

C. C. WAYLAND

is another of our successful grocery dealers. He carries a large and well assorted stock and offers an additional inducement to customers in the way of low prices. His sales during the past year indicate a growing trade.

DEY & WOLTER BRO'S

succeeded Samuel Thompson, in the grocery trade, early in the year. They have not only held the large patronage of their predecessor but have increased it. They have a specially large trade from the county, as well as their full proportion of the city custom.

M. Petersen & Son have erected a fine brick block during the past year and since they moved therein, their trade has largely increased. They are entitled to be ranked as one of the leading firms in this line.

H. Roemer engaged in the grocery October and is doing quite a prosperous business.

Rob't Scott deals in groceries, flour and feed on rather a large scale.

J. B. Carey has been engaged in business here as a vender of groceries for the past four years and is doing a snug business.

P. Lennon counts his customers by the score and therefore enjoys a liberal trade.

The remaining dealers under this head are as follows: Second Ward: D. S. Johnson, P. Heid, both of whom also handle flour and feed, and Thos. Ward. Third Ward: A. Schuldes, F. B. Franklin, A. Verhoeven, Rechner Bro's., N. Cavanaugh and John Smudde.

HARDWARE.

Our hardware houses keep pace with our general prosperity and are fully up to the demands of the town and surrounding country. Indeed, they will compare favorably with the best establishments of the kind in any interior town in the state.

BARRET & SCHLOSSER,

a firm of young men engaged in business here on the 20th of Oct., 1877. A large measure of prosperity has attended them since that time. Both of the members had the advantage of a large and desirable acquaintance and it has served them a good purpose in their enterprise. They carry an extensive stock, embracing a fine line of stoves and shelf and heavy goods. They sell at close margins and are doing a leading business in their line. Their sales for the past year are most satisfactory.

BABCOCK BRO'S.

constitute one of the oldest firms, in

their line, in the city, having been engaged here upwards of 11 years. No finer stock of goods can be found in this state and no better inducements are offered to customers anywhere than this firm presents. They sell at close margins and of course enjoy a large trade from the city and county. The extent of their annual sales entitles the firm to be ranked among the foremost in the city.

ALFRED GALPIN'S SONS

succeeded their father in business in the fall of '77 and the former prosperity of the house has attended the new administration. Their stock is a very large one, they are not undersold in Northern Wisconsin and of course do a large and prosperous busines.

The remaining firms engaged in the hardware trade but on a more limited scale are W. Findenkeller, W. E. Klœpfel and C. Fuhrberg.

GENERAL MERCHANDISE.

There are included under this head some of the leading business men and firms in the city, as will be seen from the following individual mention.

C. G. ADKINS

is emphatically the pioneer merchant in Appleton. Indeed, he antedates all other dealers now engaged in business in this city. For upwards of a quarter of a century he has been prominently identified with the mercantile trade of Appleton and his career is one eminently deserving of emulation. During all of the vicisitudes with which this period has been attended, Mr. Adkins name and credit have never suffered from a dishonorable or questionable act. He has, now and again, sustained heavy losses, but no person, either customer or dealer, has ever suffered at his hands. Financially, he is regarded as one of the soundest men in the state. He buys strictly for cash and on this account can afford to sell much lower than most competitors. He has always commanded a very large trade, both on account of the extent of his stock and the confidence which the general public has in him. Mr. Adkin's sales, during the past year are most gratifying in extent.

Chas. Mory is also one of the oldest and most extensive dealers in the city. He commands a large trade in city and country and the past year, so far as he is concerned, has been attended with reasonable success.

Mr. A. Nitchke, if the extent of his

PORTION OF THE UPPER WATER-POWER OF THE GREEN BAY AND MISSISSIPPI CANAL CO.

With Contemplated Improvements.

See page 23.

═DRUGS!═

Important Business Change.

LEWIS "THE DRUGGIST"

HAS EXPANDED INTO

LEWIS & GREULICH,

"THE DRUGGISTS."

The New Firm wish our readers, one and all,

"A Happy New Year,"

1879.

annual sales are considered, must be regarded as one of our most prominent merchants. The figures before us show that his trade during the past year, must have been very satisfactory.

K. Fischer & Son are extensive dealers, their store being located on the corner of College Avenue and Appleton Street.

CLOTHING.

There is no class of our business houses entitled to stand higher in popular estimation than our clothing establishments. Indeed, we believe the claim can be justly set up that they outrank similar concerns in any interior town in the state.

HUTCHINSON & CO.,

early in the year, changed the location of their retail department from the vicinity of their mills to 105 College Avenue, where they now occupy one of the finest stores on the street. They have also extended this branch of their business to a great extent. They have a very large custom trade and carry one of the finest assortments of cloth to be found in this part of the state. A force of 15 hands is constantly employed in the manufacturing and retail department. The firm also deals very largely in ready made clothing and all grades of woolen cloths, flannels, yarns and blankets. Their sales the past year have been surprisingly large, considering the times.

GABE ULLMAN

has been employed in business in Appleton since 1870, but engaged in his present enterprise about two years ago. That he has made a fine success of his undertaking is evident from the appearance of general thrift about his store and mammoth stock of goods. In his custom department, Gabe employs a most skillful cutter and under him are 16 workmen—this entire force being engaged in the manufacture of custom suits, than which there is none better made anywhere. Gabe's ready made stock is one of the largest in this part of the state. His sales for the year '78 show a handsome increase over the previous year.

PEERENBOOM & KOBER

are justly reckoned among our most enterprising, extensive and successful dealers. They have been engaged in business for upwards of five years and the volume of their trade has been constantly increasing. They make a specialty of custom work and indeed are engaged in all branches in their line. Their stock is unsurpassed in extent, variety and excellence and as might be expected their sales are very large.

H. A. PHINNEY

has been continually engaged in business in Appleton during the greater part of our history as a town. He is one of our most stable merchants, and commands a very extensive trade. He handles ready made goods exclusively, but his stock is very superior. Indeed he carries the best goods in the market and in point of style and durability they are seldom surpassed by custom work ; and of course he sells them at a much less figure. As his sales indicate, the past year has been a most prosperous one for Mr. Phinney.

Mr. Curren is engaged in custom tailoring and commands the trade of a large number of customers. His business is increasing from year to year.

Wm. Johnson and I. Zickler are also engaged in the same line, in the 3d ward.

JEWELERS

Appleton is abundantly provided for with jewelry establishments, and they are first-class in every respect. Indeed they would do credit to a city with 20,000 inhabitants.

M. P. GRISWOLD

has been engaged in business in Appleton upwards of five years, and during which time a reasonable measure of success has attended him. He is a royal good fellow, and it is no wonder he commands his full share of the trade. He carries a fine stock, sells at reasonable prices and is an expert workman.

JOS. SALICK & SON

have an abundance of capital and do business on a large scale. They carry as fine a stock of goods as can be found in the state outside of Milwaukee and from which, of course, the most satisfactory selections can be made. They also deal in musical instruments, and in this line as well as in their regular business they do a large trade.

CASE & FOLLET

is the style of a new firm which engaged in business in Appleton last fall. They opened out with a very choice and elegant stock of goods and by this means, as well as by their evident superior qualifications, they have made a fine impression upon the public. Their trade thus far has been most satisfactory and there is no doubt but that it will continue to increase. This firm does all kinds of repairing and engraving in a most skillful manner.

Mr. Malone is one of our oldest and most respected citizens and is doing a snug little business at his old stand.

C. F. Keller is engaged in the same line, first door west of the First National Bank.

DRUGS.

It is a matter of surprise that the city and country tributary to it can support as many first-class drug houses as we have in Appleton. As a class, they are as much of a credit to the place as the representative establishments of any other branch of trade.

H. A. FOSTER

is the oldest dealer in his line in the city, having been engaged here for upwards of 17 years. He has not only one of the finest stores in the city, but there are none in this part of the state which surpass it. It was built and furnished specially for his use. He carries an extensive and complete line of drugs, besides a great variety of other goods, commonly handled in this connection. He is one of the few merchants who buys for cash which financial capability is of great advantage to him. Mr. Foster's sales for '78 reach far into the thousands.

A. R. LEWIS

is one of the most energetic young business men in the city and never is satisfied to rank second in any enterprise in which he engages. His success in Appleton has been both marked and deserved. During the past season, he has made an important change for the better The elegant new store into which he has lately removed was erected and arranged specially for his purpose and a finer site or more attractive store is not to be found in the city. He has shown great taste and originality in furnishing it. With his increased facilities, his business has largely increased and will doubtless continue to do so.

W. F. MONTGOMERY

is doing a prosperous business in the drug line. He has an attractive store, in which a fine stock of goods are displayed. He gives special attention to the compounding of prescriptions and the preparation of various remedies. His annual sales amount to a handsome exhibit.

BENOIT & BLESSER

have a very complete store and do a large business. Their stock is as complete as any in the city and they command a large trade in the city and county. The past has been one of their most prosperous years.

FURNITURE.

Some changes have occurred in this branch of trade during the past year. But the establishments now in operation are creditable and prosperous.

A. SCHROEDER

takes the lead in this line. His stock of goods is selected with great care, is very complete and presents unusual attractions. He aims to keep down his expenses and is thus enabled to prosper on small margins with which he is contented. His sales for 1878 compare well with his most prosperous years.

FRANZ SCHREITER

succeeded Nick Simon on the first of March last. He carries a fine stock of goods and has greatly increased the trade of his predecessor. Mr. S. is a safe and thorough business man and is making a fine success of his enterprise. His sales this year present ample evidence to this effect.

Mr. C. Gierke has been engaged for some time in closing out his stock. His present place of business is near Mory's store.

BOOKS, STATIONERY, ETC.

H. H. HIMEBAUGH

is peculiarly adapted to the business in which he is engaged. He has fine taste and excellent judgment in the selection of books and the various other articles which combine to constitute a stock such as he handles. His store has special attractions during the holiday season which, this year, have proved quite irresistible. The finest productions of art and literature adorn his shelves and tables and in a cultivated community like Appleton, it is no wonder that his sales should be very large. Mr. Himebaugh's business, generally through the year, has also been quite prosperous.

H. F. HUELSTER

has proven himself to be an energetic and deserving young business man. He carries a full line of books, stationery, etc., and during the holiday season, his stock includes toys and a variety of articles for which there is a special demand at this time. Mr. H's year's sales show up well.

BOOTS AND SHOES.

If there is any branch of trade in Appleton, in advance of the public demands, it must be in the line of boots and shoes. Besides the numerous exclusive establishments many of the merchants, otherwise engaged, carry a line of these goods. However, the demands of the place are quite extensive, and the record of the year shows that our boot and shoe dealers have been quite successful. And their success would have been more marked had not numerous bankrupt and shoddy stocks been opened out here.

FAY & CLARK

constitute the leading firm, in this line in the city. They have a fine site, in the old stone block corner, and have a very large trade, in the city and country. Their stock is a very large one and embraces an assortment of the various grades of goods, adapted to the wants of the numerous classes. One advantage in dealing with this firm, and it is very material, is that the goods may always be relied upon as being as represented; and this fact the public seem to appreciate. The enterprise of this firm, coupled with their extensive facilities for supplying the wants of the public, has enabled them to reach out into neighboring towns and counties and control a large outside trade. Their sales for 1878 show a satisfactory degree of prosperity.

CHRIS ROEMER

devotes himself to manufacturing to order exclusively. He is one of the most skillful workmen in the state and many of our people refuse to be satisfied with apparel in this line unless it has passed through Chris' experienced hands. He has a very fine and desirable trade and it is constantly increasing.

Mr. Herman Bissing is one of the oldest dealers in Appleton, as he also is one of the most successful. He disposes of an enormous quantity of boots and shoes every year and finds it necessary to replenish his stock about every 30 days. His last year's business has been very successful.

A. W. Zuehlcke is an enterprising young man who does considerable business in the line of manufacturing and repairing. He is satisfied with small profits and has proved himself worthy of a liberal share of the public custom. His present place of business is at the corner of College Avenue and Morrison Street, where he has lately removed. Give him a call.

Chas Becker does a snug business both as a dealer and manufacturer. His place of business is two doors west of Patton Bros.

The other parties engaged in this line in the city are: J. F. Kaufman, C. Tchude, C. Censky, W. Becher, Rossmeisel Bros, P. C. Parish and Pat Sheel, all of whom seem to be in quite a prosperous way.

MEAT MARKETS.

GREENE & MORGAN.

opened their market on College Avenue last summer and it is a thoroughly first-class institution, in every respect. Indeed, we question if there is a better managed market in the state or one supplied with a choicer or finer variety of meats. At all events it is a decided credit to Appleton and one that meets a demand long felt. That the people appreciate the effort of this firm to cater to their tastes is evident from the extensive patronage which they are receiving. Indeed their business is vastly more of a success than they had expected. They are about opening a branch market in the 3d ward.

Fred Peterson conducts a well regulated market, being the oldest dealer in that line in the city.

Bert Harper has a market in the 2d ward and commands a large trade.

Andrew Stark has been a prosperous vender of meats during the past two years.

Louis Bonini has numerous customers and to all of whom he gives satisfaction.

The following named persons are also engaged in the marketing business: John Berg, C. Lemcke and L. Merkel & Co.

BAKERIES, ETC.

Fred. Kutler conducts the leading establishment under this head. His products are very choice and he commands a large trade.

J. L. Sutor is similarly engaged in the Petersen block.

MILLINERY, ETC.

F. A. ADSIT

has about the finest establishment that we know of in Northern Wisconsin. He has always commanded a large trade and during the past season he has more than doubled his capacity. As stated elsewhere, he has erected a fine brick block, the appointments of which are first-class in every respect, being in fact, thoroughly metropolitan in style. His store is a decided credit to the city and the fact is very gratifying that it is most liberally patronized. Mr. Adsit carries a large, superior and fashionable stock, appropriate for the season and his place is headquarters for a large number of the Appleton ladies. The past year has been a very successful one for him.

Mrs. A. Ruhlander deals in millinery and fancy goods and enjoys a very liberal patronage.

Mrs. B. Buslar is engaged in the millinery line and has quite a large trade.

Mrs. Robt. Richards is engaged in dress and cloak-making, etc., her rooms being over Pettibone's store. She is skillful in her line and enjoys an extensive patronage. There are also numerous other ladies similarly employed, but whose names we have not obtained.

PHOTOGRAPHERS.

A. Scidmore is about as skillful a photographer as can be found north of Chicago. He has an elegant gallery, over Babcock's store and finds enough to do to keep three or four hands steadily employed.

J. L. Koonz has been engaged in photographing in Appleton for upwards of 11 years. He is a skillful artist and has a large patronage.

H. F. Patton has a gallery on Oneida Street, where a fine class of pictures are turned out.

FLOUR, FEED, ETC.

H. Alexander has a store on Morrison Street, where he carries a full line of flour, feed, produce, etc. He supplies a considerable portion of the city and has a prosperous business.

M. R. Barteau deals largely in this line, his store being just north of the Post Office. He also deals in second-hand goods on quite an extensive scale.

A. Hendler does considerable business as a dealer in flour and all kinds of feed.

HARNESS MAKERS.

Ernest Heideman is a popular dealer in and manufacturer of harnesses, his shop being opposite to the office of the POST. He is a superior workman and

has a large trade in both city and county.

G. & T. Kamps are reckoned among the oldest firms in Appleton, and do a large business in harness making and dealing. They also deal extensively in hides.

C. Groth and Henry Leonhardt also are successfully engaged in this line.

CIGARS.

B. Lyons does the largest exclusive business, in this line, of any dealer in the city. He manufactures on quite a large scale, having from four to five hands constantly employed. His trade is both wholesale and retail and is quite extensive. He handles as fine a grade of goods as the market affords, and his numerous customers could hardly be satisfied with anything else. The past year has been a very successful one with Mr. Lyons.

Mrs. Silverfriend, opposite the Post Office, carries a fine line of goods and has a large trade.

L. C. Schmidt, as a manufacturer and dealer in cigars and tobacco, is doing a prosperous business.

Carl. Wickboldt and H. Tennie also command quite a large trade, in the line of tobacco and cigars.

HORSES, CATTLE, ETC.

There is a large business done, in this line in Appleton. The annual sales of the firms engaged amount to a heavy sum. D. Hammel & Co. constitute the principal firm and they import many thousands of dollars worth of horses during the year which are mostly sold to the farmers of the county. Conrad Gabel and Jacob Winefeldt deal largely in cattle—the latter also handles produce.

MARBLE WORKS.

The Powers Bros., a firm of skillful workmen, do quite a large business under this head. Their work is not surpassed by that of any firm in this part of the State. They have a fine trade in this vicinity and are rapidly extending it into the neighboring counties.

Grignon & Navarre have been engaged in business only about a year and a half but are already firmly established. Their work compares favorably with the best and they get their full proportion of orders.

MACHINERY, ETC.

O. W. Pond does a very large business

in handling reapers, mowers, seeders and farming implements in general. He represents some of the best machines in the market and his efforts in introducing them among the farmers are liberally rewarded every year.

E. C. Foster also has a large trade in the same line. He makes a specialty of the Van Brunt seeder and has sold a great number of them during the past two seasons.

Heineman & Ullman have worked up a large trade in the sewing machine line and it is constantly increasing. They represent some of the best machines.

H. W. Meyer of the *Volksfreund* also disposes of a large number of sewing machines during the course of the year.

BARBERS.

The following are the barbers who are conducting the various shops in the city: Dick. Harbeck, W. S. Cleggett, A. Lohman and Wm. Petersen.

WAGON MAKERS AND BLACK-SMITHS.

Until the present year, Wm. Pardee has done quite a large business in the manufacture of carriages, cutters and light work in general, but lately there has been so much inferior work brought into the city and disposed of here, that it has interfered with his trade considerably. Of course, his work being strictly first-class, he could not compete in price with these shoddy productions. Mr. Pardee is one of the most skillful and thorough mechanics and when a person gets one of his vehicles he is sure of something both stylish and durable. A little more experience will impress this fact upon the people. On account of the reason stated, Mr. Pardee is now devoting himself principally to general blacksmithing.

James Monroe is still engaged in the manufacture of carriages and a variety of light work and continues to be successful. He is a skillful mechanic and his work is strictly first-class.

Chris Heinz is as industrious as ever in the manufacture of wagons and general blacksmithing. Chris. is a thorough workman and his products are as good as the market affords.

Wm. Voge and Bernhard Utuheimar are also doing a successful business in wagon making and blacksmithing.

As heretofore, J. W. Bedell divides his time in pounding at the anvil and obeying the behests of the muses. The following named persons are also engaged in blacksmithing: Jas. Pardee, M. Champagne, A. Klein, Jas. Tilford, Kaster & Hæbig, A. Schweuzfeir, Louis St. James and Charley Horr.

LIVERYMEN.

J. D. Flack has one of the most complete livery stables in Northern Wisconsin. Its appointments are first-class throughout, the rigs being stylish, safe and comfortable. During the past year, Mr. Flack purchased the stable and property which he occupies—it being the best site for this purpose in the city. As might be expected, he has a very large patronage.

Last summer Peter Steenis bought an interest in the stable on Johnson Street and the firm is now Siekman & Steenis. Their stable is abundantly supplied with the best class of rigs and the firm is doing a paying business.

During the past year, P. J. Gates bought out A. H. Perkins and the former is now running a first-class livery, in the rear of the Manufacturer's Bank.

Comerford & Shinners have a stable on Appleton Street and Fose & Co. have one on Morrison Street.

PRINTING.

Ryan & Bro. have been the continuous publishers of the *Crescent* for over a quarter of a century. This is confessedly one of the best conducted local papers in the state and enjoys a liberal support. The firm also does a general job printing business, for which they have excellent facilities, including a fine assortment of type, steam presses and other modern appliances.

H. W. Meyer publishes the *Volksfreund*, one of the ablest and most widely circulated German papers in the state. He also does quite a large business in the line of job printing. He has a most complete office, including two presses which are run by steam.

G. E. Mendel is the publisher of the "Appleton Globe" and it is hoped, on account of his misfortunes, makes a comfortable living.

The *Collegian* is a liberally sustained monthly, published by the college students. It is a very creditable representative of Lawrence University and is ably conducted.

Wolter & Johnson have lately engaged in the job printing line. They have quite a complete little office and will, no doubt, do well.

The Post Publishing Co., publishers of this paper, suffered a heavy loss one year ago, in the complete destruction of their office by fire. But they have since recovered and now have as fine and complete an office as there is in Northwestern Wisconsin—the type being all new and of the latest styles. They have three steam presses and other first-class facilities for doing handsome, rapid and cheap work.

RESTAURANTS.

Within the last few weeks, W. Hinchliff bought out A. H. Perkins and has since been running a first class restaurant.

Geo. Ball succeeded Frank Wright last summer and now conducts the leading restaurant in the city, over Gabe Ullman's store. He is largely patronized.

MILK & VEGETABLES.

W. H. Rogers does a very large dairy business and also raises vegetables on a large scale. His farm is situated, just outside of the city, on the banks of Fox River, and is a most productive tract of land. His products are disposed of, by daily visits, among the residents of the city.

M. B. Johnson supplies a very large number of patrons in the city with milk, every day. His business appears to be profitable and is constantly increasing.

CONTRACTORS, BUILDERS, ETC.

Contractors.—Appleton has numerous and competent skilled mechanics, classed as above, among whom the following stand at the head. Thos. O'Keefe, Schneider & Wilson, H. G. Ashman, Wm. Johnson, Mr. Record, Lewis Bates, W. H. Packard, J. W. Caboon, Christian Loth, A. A. Barron, D. G. Stowe and J. B. Brown.

Painters.—The leading workmen belonging to this class are: Gallagher & Hanchett, Jim McCabe, N. Jensen, Liew Cole and Henry Bielenberg.

OMNIBUS LINES AND DRAYMEN.

Omnibus Lines.—Under this head, Geo. W. Turner and Wm. Johnson do the business of the city.

Draymen.—The following named persons are always ready for a job in their line : S. S Sheldon, Bert Reynolds, J. F. Merril, Carl Breening, Chas. Bentley, J. S. Wells and P..J. Gates.

SALOONS, BREWERIES, ETC.

Under this head, the aggregate slaes are considerably larger this year than last.

Carl Muench, one of the leading brewers in Northwestern Wisconsin, does a very large business over in the Fourth Ward. During the past year he has expended $6,000 in buildings and improvements. His sales, during this time, amount to $15,000.

M. Freis conducts quite a successful brewery in the Third Ward, and Wm. Wendels & Son are similarly engaged in the Second Ward.

Our minutes show that there are 17 different saloons in the city besides six other places where liquor is sold in connection with other business. According to careful calculations the aggregate sales for the year amount to about $31,-000.

MISCELLANEOUS.

E. N. Johnson conducts a first-class hat and cap store and gents' furnishing establishment. His place of business is with Hutchinson & Co. Eb. engaged in this line last summer and has already secured a large trade.

Arnold Alexander has been dealing quite largely in the same line but is now closing out, with the view of engaging in business in Chicago.

Geo. Vatter has the only exclusive lamp house and fixtures and gas fitting establishment in the city. He carries a superb line of lamp goods and has lately reduced his prices 50 per cent. from the usual rates. His assortment is as fine and extensive as can be found in the state and of cou rse the most satisfactory selections can be made from his stock. As a gas fitter and plumber he is skillful and accurate and is always employed when there is work of this kind to be done.

Frank Wohlman conducts an exclusive notion establishment and carries an extensive stock of goods. Frank sells at very moderate prices and has a large trade.

Louis Lehman is the only ice dealer in the city and of course has a large trade during the summer season.

F. B. Voight deals extensively in leather and hides. His sales for the year show a prosperous business.

N. W. Martin is proprietor of the lumber yard near the depot. He has quite an extensive stock and enjoys a liberal patronage

F. W. Feiker is the only book binder in the city and finds work enough to do to keep several hands steadily employed. His bindery is in the rear of Warner & Ryan's office.

J. Hannauer is a practical gunsmith and is a skillful mechanic as well. He also carries quite a large stock of hunter's weapons and materials and has a liberal patronage.

R. C. Kruschke has a second hand store, near the ravine and has quite a clever business.

Anton Shaller conducts a general repair shop in the 2nd ward.

A. Vohl does a large business in hotel keeping and merchandising. He also has a saloon attached. His place is headquarters for many of the farmers.

The following named persons are engaged in keeping boarding houses—some of them also dealing in groceries: J. Speaker, J. McCarthy, Jos. Burk and John Nolan.

PROFESSIONAL.

Lawyers.—The bar of Appleton probably ranks higher than that of any town in the state, of equal size. It contains men of ability, experience and fine reputation, throughout the state, as well as in this immediate locality; also numerous young man of marked talents and promise. The following individuals and firms are engaged in business here: Geo. H. Myers, Collins & Pierce, Bottensek & Harriman, Barnes & Goodland, Wm. Kennedy, Patchin, Weed & Lester, S. Baird, Samuel Boyd, D. C. Babcock, Foster, Davis & Foster, W. J. Allen, H. C. Sloan and A. H. Kellog.

Physicians.—Appleton has a large number of physicians and most of them have a very successful practice. This profession in this city includes a high order of talent which is known and recognized throughout the state. The persons engaged in the practice of medicine are as follows:

J. T. Reeve, E. Stansbury, Rush Winslow, A. H. Levings, M. F. Page, Dr. Von Heidesson, J. R. Reilly, Miss P. D. Bullock, John Sutherland, Dr. Long and Dr. Heideman, of the Northwestern Surgical Institute.

Dentists.—This profession is ably represented in Appleton, in the persons of Dr. Chilson, Dr. Douglas and Douglas & Buck.

Justices of the Peace.—Justice is equitably administered in Appleton by S. P. Ming, Sam Ryan, Jr., and A. W. Ballard.

Civil Engineers, Milwrights, etc. —The following named persons are engaged in the professions indicated: O. A. Byrns, millwright; J.M. Barker, Civil Engineer; Chas. Gillette and E. Spencer, Surveyors.

RECAPITULATION.

To show, in a brief space, what has been done, in the city, the past year, under the various foregoing heads, we herewith present a complete recapitulation, which is as accurate as labor and unusual care could make it:

Boots and Shoes	$ 82,400
Books, Stationery, etc	15,300
Bakery and Confectionery	8,000
Blacksmithing, wagon making, etc	21,500
Barbers	6,000
Building, Contracting, etc	61,000
Clothing	89,000
Cigars, Tobacco, etc	28,500
Cattle, Horses, etc	61,000
Dry Goods	300,000
Drugs	56,000
Draying and Omnibus lines	8,000
Flour, Feed, etc	43,500
Furniture	33,000
General Merchandise	140,000
Groceries	215,000
Gas	12,000
Hardware	94,500
Harnesses, etc	24,000
Hotels	73,500
Jewelers	24,000
Liveries	27,500
Millinery	26,000
Meat Markets	60,500
Marble Works	12,000
Machinery, etc	29,000
Milk, Vegetables, etc	11,000
Miscellaneous	144,000
Printing	26,000
Photographs	7,000
Restaurants	5,000
Saloons, Breweries, etc	52,000
Professional	64,000
Total	1,770,200

MUNICIPAL

NUMEROUS INTERESTING FACTS UNDER THIS HEAD, BECAUSE THEY TOUCH THE POCKETS
OF THE PEOPLE—WHAT HAS BEEN DONE IN THE WAY OF PUBLIC IMPROVEMENTS DUR-
ING THE YEAR—THE EXPENSE REQUIRED TO MAINTAIN THE VARIOUS DEPARTMENTS
INDICATED IN DETAIL—STATISTICAL TABLES SHOWING THE DISBURSEMENTS FOR THE
YEAR AND FOR WHAT PURPOSE—A COMPREHENSIVE STATEMENT SHOWING OUR FINAN-
CIAL CONDITION.

IMPROVEMENTS.

The efforts of our present city government, during the past year, have been
principally directed towards keeping
down our expenses to the lowest possible gauge compatible with public interests; and if our local rulers are entitled to any verdict at the hands of the
people, it is that they have succeeded,
in this respect, to a very respectable extent. Still, no important matter has
been neglected, and every question involving the public weal has received due
consideration at their hands. In a
young, thriving and rapidly growing city
like Appleton, a considerable expenditure is required every year. Besides the
various departments having demands upon the public treasury and which the
common good and the credit of the
municipality require to be maintained,
there are numerous streets which need
improving, new thoroughfares to be
opened, bridges to be built and repaired,
walks to be constructed and various other
purposes involving considerable expenditure.

During the past season, as will be
seen the disbursements, for all purposes
are about the same as presented in our
last Annual Review. And the past year,
the same as the year previous, the expenditures on our public thoroughfares
have been for the purpose of making repairs rather than the accomplishment of
new work. That this policy meets with
general approval, there is no doubt, on
account of the general distress which
prevails throughout the country and from
which Appleton is not entirely separated.
We particularize below the more important work which has been accomplished:

A considerable improvement has been
made on South Division Street, abutting
the most populous part of the Fourth
Ward. Grade lines have been established and the street constructed in con-
formity therewith. The amount expended to accomplish this work is
$92.00.

Maine Street, in the Fourth Ward,

has also been similarly improved, at an
expense of $95.00. This street is in an
important section of the city and the
improvement mentioned will add considerably to its general utility.

A very important work has been done
on South River Street, in the Third
Ward, viz: the construction of substantial stone walls on the south line of this
street and dividing it from the canal in
that vicinity and the yards of the Atlas
Paper Co. This work was necessary to
the permanent protection of the street
and the expenditure required for this
purpose, amounting to $280.00, was jus-
tifiable. But this sum represents only
one-half of the outlay—the Paper Co.
joining the city in this work and shar-
ing equally in the expense.

A culvert was built on Green
Street, in the First Ward, at an expense
of $185.00. The structure is a very dur-
able one and will be of service now and
hereafter when the improvements contemplated are made.

The past year a sewer has been built
on Lawrence Street, in the Third Ward,
requiring an outlay of $201.26. This
work was very necessary and important
as it furnishes drainage facilities to a
part of the city which suffered somewhat heretofore.

All of the other work which has been
done the past year has been under the
supervision of the Street Commissioner,
acting under directions of the Common
Council. We herewith submit a statement showing the disbursements by
months, in this manner:

AMOUNT EXPENDED ON STREETS,
BRIDGES, ETC.

January	$ 66.85
February	48.85
March	251.74
April	191.58
May	210.24
June	608.80
July	657.77
August	336.28
September	427.83
October	750.88
November	737.99
December	336.00
Total for the year	$4,624.81

SUPPORT OF THE POOR.

This is always a considerable tax upon every municipality, but in civilized communities it is one of the first duties of society. In Appleton, the question receives due attention and every needy and deserving case is carefully looked after. Mr. J. P. Hawley has shown himself to be a most efficient person to have charge of this department. The following figures show the disbursements, by months, under this head, including the salary of the poor master ($150) and keeper of poor house ($360):

January	$ 132.50
February	126.21
March	195.17
April	145.32
May	147.98
June	120.26
July	138.36
August	99.60
September	100.64
October	118.32
November	101.32
December	142.50
Total	$1,568.17
Decrease from 1877,	$ 362.12

FIRE DEPARTMENT.

Appleton has as well a regulated and efficient fire department as any city in the State, in proportion to its size. We have two excellent engine houses, one in the Second and one in the Third Ward. These are provided with all of the conveniences calculated to secure the greatest effectiveness. We also have two first-class fire steamers, together with the necessary appurtenances and which are fully equal to any emergency which is likely to arise, especially when we consider the fact that they are in the hands of companies the members of which may almost be classed as experts. Both organizations have and are serving the city faithfully and well, in protecting its property against the ravages of fire. The present officers of the department are

O. A. BYRNS, *Chief Engineer.*
C. V. ADKINS, *First Ass't Engineer.*
E. T. CONKEY, *Second Ass't Engineer.*
PHILLIP WOELLER, *Third Ass't Engineer.*
THOS. O'KEEFE, *Secretary.*
C. C. WAYLAND, *Treasurer.*

Considering the benefits secured the expense of our fire department is as light as could be expected. For the year now closed it has been as follows, including the salaries of the firemen, viz., $10.00 each:

January	$ 416.75
February	168.59
March	274.77
April	123.00
May	190.83
June	211.20
July	112.11

August	257.66
September	108.45
October	221.57
November	485.90
December	240.00
Total for the year	$2,810.83
Decrease from 1878	$1.104.73

NOTE.—The city purchased one span of horses and a set of double harness, the past year, for the use of the department, at an expense of $363.

SALARIES OF OFFICES.

There is no servant of the city which receives a munificent reward for his labors indeed hardly as much as the same labor would command if privately employed, and yet the tax-payers have never been heard to complain. The following figures show what has been paid out to salaried officers, during the year, including special policemen and City Engineer, but excluding Fire Wardens, Street Commissioner, Poormaster, City Treasurer and Engineers of Steamers:

January	$ 254.84
February	140.17
March	230.33
April	194.25
May	265.50
June	559.50
July	628.50
August	438.75
September	244.50
October	549.25
November	232.00
December	230.00
Total for the year	$3,967.59
Decrease from 1877	$1,043.98

PRINTING.

The city has paid out the following amounts for the necessary public printing during the year:

January	$285.00
February	37.00
March	23.70
April	56.10
May	36.17
June	53.74
July	37.20
August	74.49
September	54.41
October	108.14
November	89.38
December	56.00
Total	$911.33
Increase over 1877	$ 46.89

NOTE.—Part of the amount paid for month of January was for printing 1,000 copies of the Charter and Ordinances of the city, ($257.)

BOARD OF REGISTRY AND ELECTION.

The following is what it has cost the citizens of Appleton to exercise the inestimable right of the elective franchise during the year 1878:

May	$125.00
November	224.00
December	32.00
Total	381.00

GAS.

The city has been a liberal consumer of this beautiful illuminator during the year, but few will say that the cost therefor has not been largely compensated in the embellished appearance which our streets have presented at night and in the real practical benefits which have been derived—especially as the actual expense to the people, over and above the tax paid by the gas corporation, is less than $300. The following appropriations were made for gas and expenses thereon, including lamp lighters wages:

January	84.20
February	68.00
March	62.20
April	55.90
May	380.62
June	41.00
July	40.45
August	42.55
September	58.75
October	68.65
November	86.07
December	70.80
Total for the year	$1,059.19

NOTE.—Part of the amount paid for month of May was for all the street lamp posts, globes and fixtures—$334.02.

MISCELLANEOUS.

Under this head are included all items of disbursements which are not properly included in any of the foregoing statements:

January	$ 131.75
February	152.58
March	277.26
April	144.57
May	317.32
June	83.81
July	5.57
August	35.61
September	295.68
October	364.32
November	171.92
December	17.50
Total for the year	$1,997.89

RECAPITULATION.

That the reader may determine at a glance what our current expenses for the year 1878 has been and what they were made for we herewith submit a recapitulation of the foregoing:

Streets, bridges, etc	$ 5,477.83
Support of the poor	1,568.18
Fire department	2,810.83
Salaries of officers	3,967.59
Printing	911.33
Election purposes	381.00
Gas, fixtures, lamp lights, &c	1,059.19
Miscellaneous	1,997.89
Total for the year	$18,173.84
Decrease from 1877	2,058.11

REDUCING THE DEBT.

The city of Appleton is prompt, as it should be, in discharging its financial obligations. Provisions have been made in the recent tax levy to meet certain claims upon us which mature in February and March and which are as follows:

Fire loan bonds	$ 1,000.00
coupons	280.00
C. & N. W. R. R. coupons	70.00
Grand Chute Pl'k Road bonds	1,750.00
Funding bill bonds	4,000.00
coupons	280.00
A. & N. L. R. R. coupons	5,250.00
Total	$12,630.00

STATE AND COUNTY.

The following are the city's proportion of the state and county tax and, together with the other items named, will be paid out of the revenue of 1878:

State tax	$ 3,646.13
County tax	7,274.00
" judgment tax	192.00
" school tax	1,000.00
Total	$12,112.23

DUE SCHOOL DISTRICTS.

The following amounts will be paid to the several districts for the coming year:

School District No. 1 tax	$ 1,800.00
" " " 2 "	7,835.00
" " " 3 "	3,579.00
" " " 4 "	2,650.00
Total	$15,864.00

RECAPITULATION.

Amount Received.

The revenue received from all sources during the year is as follows:

General tax levy	$64,986.89
Licenses, amusements, etc	2,413.62
Total	$67,400.51
Increase over 1877	6,335.71

Amount Expended.

The following is a general statement of expenditures and for what purpose they were made:

General expenses	$18,173.84
Bonds and interest	12,630.00
State and county tax	12,112.23
District school tax	15,864.00
Total expenditures for the year	$58,780.07

OUR PUBLIC DEBT.

The following table is a correct statement of all our liabilities, what they consist of and when they fall due:

C. & N. W. R. R. bonds	$ 1,000	Feb. 1, 1880
Fire loan bonds	1,000	" 1, 1879
" " "	1,000	" 1, 1880
" " "	1,000	" 1, 1881
" " "	1,000	" 1, 1882
G. C. Pl'k Road bonds	25,000	" 10, 1893
Funding bill bonds	4,000	Mch. 1, 1879
A. & N. L. R. R. bonds	75,000	Feb. 1, 1891
Interest due	7,630	
Total	$116,630	

The Appleton and New London Railroad bonds mature as follows:

$2,000 due Feb. 1st, 1880.
$3,000 in each year from 1881 to 1890 inclusive.
$43,000 due Feb. 1st, 1891.

All of the foregoing bonds bear interest at the rate of 7% per annum.

It will be noticed above that, of this amount, the payment of $12,630 has been provided for this year, in the general tax levy. This will reduce the total city debt to $104,000.

ASSESSED VALUATION.

The assessed valuation of property in Appleton is as follows:

Total Real Estate................$1,427,240.00
Total personal................... 409,680.00

Grand total...................$1,833,920.00
Increase over 1877............. 276,109.00

REMARKS.

It has been the policy of the present, as well as past administrations, to maintain the credit of the city, both at home and abroad, at a high standard. This has been accomplished by wise and prudent legislation. The importance of a healthy financial status cannot be overestimated. It adds greatly to the splendid reputation which our city enjoys otherwise abroad and is particularly creditable by contrast if we consider the efforts which are being put forth by many western towns (including some of our neighbors) to repudiate their financial obligations. Appleton has not a dollar of paper outstanding which is not worth its face and which will not be promptly and fully paid when the same falls due. And that her present good name will be preserved and guarded with a jealous care is the determination of her people.

CITY OFFICERS.

The personnel of our city government is, at present, as follows:

Mayor—James Ryan,
Clerk—P. J. Cirkel.
Attorney—H. C. Sloan.
Treasurer—Joseph Koffend.
Marshal—James Golden.
Engineer—J. M. Barker.
Street Commissioner—S. D. Walsh.
Assessors—A. B. Randall, Jno. Goodland and Geo. Schuldez.

ALDERMEN.

First Ward—Chase Prescott and Jno. Bottensek.
Second Ward—Chris. Heinz and S. K. Wambold.
Third Ward—C. C. Wayland and Humphrey Pierce.
Fourth Ward—John Bauer and John Ryan.
Fifth Ward—F. Schreiter and Chris. Roemer.
Sixth Ward—C. Tschude and R. S. Baird.

BUILDING AND IMPROVEMENTS.

WHAT HAS BEEN ACCOMPLISHED IN THIS RESPECT DURING THE YEAR NOW CLOSED—THE EXHIBIT, IN AGGREGATE FORM, BEING A POTENT INDICATION OF THE CITY'S PROSPERITY—THE PRINCIPAL OUTLAYS MADE WHERE THEY WILL DO THE MOST GOOD, VIZ: ON AND ALONG THE RIVER—ALSO SOME FINE BUSINESS BLOCKS ERECTED AS WELL AS SEVERAL HANDSOME RESIDENCES—MINOR IMPROVEMENTS, ETC., ETC.

As one evidence of the growth and progress of Appleton, we never fail to present, in our Annual Reviews, facts relating to what has been accomplished, during the previous year, in the way of building and improvements. And the data which 1878 has furnished us are fully as gratifying, as the exhibit of any previous year. In fact, all things considered, they are even more flattering. Of course, in considering what has been done, the fact must not be lost sight of that the whole country is still depressed, in consequence of not having escaped from the great financial revulsion, beginning in 1873. Also that but few towns in the west have made any considerable progress during the intervening time, and these only the most fortunately located and highly favored. The rule has been a period of retrogression rather than advancement. And yet a stranger to the events of the past five years, visiting this locality any time during the season which has now closed, would never suspect from the indications here, but that the country was passing through one of its eras of greatest prosperity. There has been general activity on every hand, in the way of building and improvements. This fact has attracted great attention to Appleton and has caused its fame as a thriving young city to reach far and wide. The conclusion has been generally and wisely reached that a town that can successfully stem the tide of "hard times" possesses advantages rarely enjoyed.

A fact in connection with this part of our work which is especially gratifying is that the bulk of our expenditures during the past year have been made upon our water power--in the establishment of new industries and the enlargement of those previously in operation. This is of the greatest consequence, as the development of our resources for manufacturing is at the basis of all our prosperity. As will be seen farther on, the outlays in this respect have been very large and have secured the most important results. But the upbuilding and the improvement of the city in other respects have not been neglected. In fact, a great deal has been done. Some very fine business blocks have been erected, as well as numerous attractive residences.

The amount expended in improvements will also compare favorably with the advancement of previous years. We have collected as complete data for this Annual Review, as on previous occasions, but we omit some of the details heretofore presented. But the aggregate result is what is important, and the figures upon which that is based may be relied upon as being as correct as if separately presented.

ON THE WATER-POWER.

We omit here the details of expenditures made on our water power, in new buildings and improvements as they are elsewhere fully set forth, but we present in the final summing up, the figures showing the total disbursements for this purpose.

BUSINESS BLOCKS.

College Avenue, our principal business street, has undergone few but very important changes this season. But little, however could be expected, on account of the large amount of building done hitherto and within recent years. Indeed but little more than ten years have elapsed since the first brick building was erected, on this street, and now but few others are to be seen. Our business blocks are all first class and compare favorably with the buildings in other and older and more pretentious cities.

During the past season, J. A. Bertschy erected a magnificent block which would be a credit to the metropolis of the state. The first floor, which is twice the size of the average store, is occupied by A. D. Fleming & Co., who present a cut of this block elsewhere. The building is ad-

mirable in design and is handsomely finished outside and in. It cost $8,000.

Pettibone & Co. were compelled by their rapidly increasing trade to add considerably to the size of their store the past year. The addition is in keeping with the original block and represents an outlay of $2,000.

Geo. Kreiss has erected an elegant brick store, on the south east corner of College Avenue and Oneida Street. It is one of the finest business blocks in the city and its erection involved an outlay of $5,000.

F. A. Adsit has done an important work, this season, which adds materially to the appearance of the Avenue. He has virtually rebuilt his block and now has a most attractive business place. His expenditures for the year amount to $3,000.

Peterson & Son have erected a very handsome brick block on College Avenue this season which represents an outlay of $4,000. It compares favorably in appearance with the best of our business structures.

Squire Bateman, Mr. Ware and F. P. Voight have each added one story to their buildings on College Avenue which greatly improves the appearance thereof, besides adding to their utility. Their combined outlay is about $1800,

Henry Wendelborn has put up a brick building, on Appleton street, on the first lot north of the Waverly House which is in keping with our best class of buildings. It cost $2,500.

Miscellaneous improvements, throughout the business part of the city, and of which we have caused careful estimates to be made, have been acomplished at a total expense of $7,000. We omit the details on account of the great demand for space which our work this week involves. In the aggregate no item is included which does not exceed $150.

RESIDENCES AND IMPROVEMENTS THERON.

Previous years have witnessed the expenditures of larger sums of money than the present in the erection of private residences. But that is because most of our leading business men had already amply provided for their wants in this direction. However, there has been something accomplished in 1878 in this direction. A few excellent dwellings have been erected while the improvements on this class of property has been quite extensive.

Mr. J. W. Hammond has put up one of the most attractive residences in the city in the First Ward, on John Street. It is large, conveniently planned and well finished outside and in. Indeed, nothing has been neglected to make it a pleasant home. Its cost was $4,000.

Judge Myers has also erected an elegant dwelling on the corner of Lawrence and Morrison Streets. It is made up of old parts but these have been so thoroughly overhauled as to render the structure practically new. The Judge has now a most attractive home and long may he live to enjoy it. His improvements, this year, cost about $3,000.

Dr. Levings has rebuilt his residence on College Avenue, First Ward, on quite an elaborate scale, and now has as fine a homestead as that part of the city affords. The Dr. has expended about $2,000 to secure this result.

The above are the principal items under this head. There have been, however, numerous smaller residences erected, throughout the city, and various important improvements and enlargements have also been made. The data before us, which has been carefully collected, show that the total amount of expenditures, exclusive of the above, aggregate to $14,000.

OTHER BUILDINGS.

Specially deserving of note, under this head, is the Fourth Ward School House which was erected quite late, this season. It is the finest school edifice in the city and when fully completed, it will be an ornament to the ward in which it is situated. It will cost, when completed, about $7,000.

Mr. Carl Meunch has erected a mammoth store house, near his brewery in the Fourth Ward. It is 36x70 feet and three stories high. It is built of brick and in appearance is one of the best buildings in the city. This building represents an outlay of $6,000.

RECAPITULATION OF BUILDING AND IMPROVEMENTS.

Total expended on water power.	...$164,900
Total expended on business blocks,	32,800
Total expended on residences, etc.,	23,000
Total expended on others.	13,000
Grand Total	$233,700

We need not occupy further space in commenting upon this subject. The figures speak eloquently in their own behalf and of the present prosperity of our city. Indeed we questson if there is another town in the west which can show proportionately as fine a record of advancement for the year as Appleton. In any event, however, our people, ambitious as they are, have a right to be satisfied with this faithful exhibit which we have presented.

A CHAPTER OF MISCELLANY.

IN WHICH ARE INCLUDED NUMEROUS AND VERY IMPORTANT ENTERPRISES—OUR BANKS—HOTELS—GAS WORKS—REAL ESTATE—INSURANCE—BUSINESS DONE AT THE TELEGRAPH, EXPRESS AND POST OFFICES—THE SURGICAL INSTITUTE.

BANKS.

Banks are among the most useful enterprises which can be found in any community. Indeed, regarded as labor saving institutions alone, society has long since passed that point where it has come to regard them as quite indispensible. Being the depository of the wealth of nations they are relied upon to perform the important function of supplying the facilities for trade. Indeed they are the institutions, more than any other, which distinguish a civilized from a barborous people. In the latter case, trade can only be accomplished by exchanging one product for another and that can

only be done, at a great sacrifice of time and labor—each producer being compelled to seek a customer which possesses the articles which he desires and who is willing to exchange them for what his neighbor has to offer therefor. But with a monetary system, of which banks are at once the outgrowth, as well as representative institutions, means are furnished into which all kinds of products can be converted, to the mutual advantage of all, and at a great saving to each individual class. Moreover, they are the places where the treasurers of the millionaire and the saving of the poor alike obtain security and revenue and where the enterprising business man can secure the accommodation necessary to enable him to conduct his business successfully. It has been reserved for our day and the American people to regard banking institutions as an unmixed evil, but this is the result of false and vicious teaching and the notion must soon pass away with advancing enlightenment. At all events, we are glad to be able to say that Appleton is favored with ample banking facilities.

THE FIRST NATIONAL BANK

has been in operation for the past eight years. The building which it now occupies was erected by the corporation for its purposes in 1872. It is situated on the corner of College Avenue and Appleton street and is a substantial, convenient and handsome structure. It is provided with burglar and fire proof vaults and furnishes as thorough security for its patrons as human ingenuity can contrive. The corporation is made up of our leading business men who are recognized at home and abroad, as men of prudence, integrity and sound financial ability. The directors of the institution are: Aug. Ledyard Smith, G. W. Spaulding, E. C. Goff, W. G. Whorton, J. T. Reeve and Welcome Hyde. And the officers of this bank are as follows: Aug. Ledyard Smith, Pres.; E. C. Goff, Vice Pres.; Herman Erb, Cashier. On account of the excellent management of the First National, it is no wonder that it enjoys the confidence of the public in a marked degree. For this reason, it has always done the leading banking business in this city. It has passed through some trying ordeals, but it has never suffered from the loss of an iota of public confidence, and neither, on the other hand, have its patrons ever sustained the slightest financial misfortune at its hands, and no business man, when presenting the proper security, has ever been denied an accommodation which he had any right to expect. To show the present condition of the First National, Mr. Erb, by request, has furnished us with the following special statement.

RESOURCES.

Bills discounted,	$145,854.02.
Cash on hand	23,083.28.
U. S. Bonds on hand	300.00.
Real Estate,	12,000.00.
U. S. Securities,	50,000.00.
Redemption fund,	2,250.00.
Due from other banks,	11,409.02.
Total,	$247,396.00.

LIABILITIES.

Deposits,	$62,902.28.
Bills rediscounted,	3,200.00.
Circulation,	45,000.00.
Profit and Loss,	5,586.94.
Surplus,	15,000.00.
Due to Banks,	10,707.20.
Total,	247,396.35.

THE MANUFACTURERS' NATIONAL BANK.

This institution was organized in 1871, and its history thus far has been most satisfactory and deservedly prosperous. The building which it now occupies was erected in 1874 and is one of the finest of its class in the state, being situated on the corner of College Avenue and Morrison Street. It was erected specially for the purpose for which it is being used, is elegantly furnished and supplied with the most perfect fire proof vaults and safe. The former has a Yaletime lock attached, the object of which is to render the "bulldozing" of the Cashier wholly unprofitable and useless. By means of this device, the vaults can only be opened at a certain hour, even by one in possession of the combination. Of course such an arrangement adds to the security of the bank as a place of deposit.

The management of the Manufacturers' Bank is also in the hands of men in whom the public has the utmost confidence. They are careful conservative and sagacious and are men of known integrity and financial responsibility. The stockholders include some of the best men in the city. The officers of the corporation are as follows: C. G. Adkins, Prest.; Alfred Galpin, Jr., Cashier.

The Manufacturers' Bank does a large business and the volume thereof is constantly increasing. The following figures will shed considerable light on this point:

Capital	$ 50,000.00
Surplus	6,100.00
Deposits	65,000.00
Exchange sold during the year..	500,000.00
Silver coin paid out as change...	6,000.00

HOTELS.

While, of course, there are numerous points which determine the character and reputation of a city, locally and generally, there are none that figure with greater importance, than the hotel accommodations which it affords. Indeed strangers and all transient visitors receive their impressions almost wholly from this source and often times questions of great moment to a city are determined upon this basis. Fortunately for Appleton, it is blessed with ample facilities of this kind and of a character, too, that will compare favorably with those possessed by older and larger cities.

THE WAVERLY HOUSE

is unquestionably one of the finest hotels in the interior of the State, and the very best, all things considered, of any located on the C. & N. W. R. R., north of Chicago. It is a mammoth four story brick building, of which the following is an illustration :

The Waverly is located on the corner of Appleton and Lawrence Streets, convenient enough to the business center to answer every purpose, and just far enough removed to have beautiful surroundings and to avoid the rattle of business activity. The rooms are all well lighted and ventillated and are as cheerful as any public house can contain. Moreover they are comfortably and handsomely furnished and their attractions, in every way, are all that the traveling public could desire.

The Waverly has become noted for its bills of fare and the surprise of many of its patrons is that they can be made so elaborate in an interior town, where market facilities are, of necessity, more or less limited. And they are served in true metropolitan style which always adds materially to the gratification of its guests.

The proprietor of the Waverly, Mr. W. H. Cottrill, is one of the most experienced and competent landlords in the Northwest. He has had charge of some of the best and largest hotels in the West and understands thoroughly what will best please his customers in the way of accommodations. He makes his business the subject of the most careful study and neglects no labor or expense to provide the most complete accommodations and entertainment for his guests.

He employs the most skilled help that can be found in his culinary department and the results of their handiwork is visible three times every day. Mr. Cottrill is a most courteous and obliging manager and it is therefore no wonder that all patrons of the Waverly are his personal friends as well. We consider it most fortunate for Appleton that we have such a man at the head of our hotel interests.

THE BRIGGS HOUSE.

This hotel was leased last summer, by Mr. A. Townsend, one of the old, well known and popular landlords in Northern Wisconsin. "Lot" has fairly revolutionized the Briggs House since he became manager. Consulting the convenience and comforts of his guests, he has made numerous important improvements which will contribute largely to this end. The rooms are well furnished, and comfortable and attractive. But it is the table which is the chief attraction of the Briggs House and which largely determine its excellent standing with the public. Although the accommodations of the Briggs House are all that we have represented, the fare is only one-half of that usually charged, viz., $1.00 per day. It is therefore no wonder that the patronage of the House is considerably increasing.

THE NORTHWESTERN HOUSE,

of which Mr. A. Hettinger is the proprietor, is one of the institutions of the city. The building is a substantial, handsome and extensive one and is situated on Appleton Street, between the Avenue and the depot. Louis furnishes excellent accommodations for the traveling public, both as regards table and rooms. He is largely patronized by transient customers and also has an extensive trade from the country, for which class his place is special headquarters. Mr. Hettinger also conducts a store and saloon in connection with his hotel. He is reckoned among the most prosperous men of the place.

E. H. Stone conducts the Lawrence House in the Third Ward and has quite a large patronage.

Geo. Kreiss and J. Nicklaus are each engaged in the hotel business and have a considerable trade in that line.

GAS WORKS.

The gas works, in Appleton, have now been in operation something over one year. They are the most complete institution of the kind, in the entire state. The buildings are substantial and all the other work also strictly first class. The very best quality of gas is furnished and the enterprise is being liberally patronized. About 10,000 feet are being consumed nightly. Now that our people have had a taste of the luxury afforded by this illuminator, they could not be persuaded to get along without it.

REAL ESTATE.

Appleton has numerous men of extensive means, engaged in handling real estate. The past year, however, as well as two or three preceeding that, has been most unfavorable, here and elsewhere, for this business. The demands have been limited and the purchases have also been considerably limited.

Welcome Hyde is probably the most extensive dealer, in this line, in the city. He has large interests here, but the bulk of his investments are in pine, farming and mineral lands, variously located throughout Northern Wisconsin. He has made considerable many purchases during the year and some very important sales, reaching well into the thousands.

Humphrey Pierce has extensive real estate interests in Appleton, including some of the choicest property in the city. As soon at there is a change in the times, he will have no difficulty in making frequent and important sales.

Judge Harriman has been largely engaged in handling real estate during the past five years, and he allows no season to pass without making extensive improvements. The past year has been no exception with him. Indeed he has probably made more expenditures during 1878 than any other dealer.

W. S. Warner is one of our heaviest real estate owners, both in and outside of the city. He does a large business every year, in buying and selling, His transactions for 1878 show up well, considering the times.

Reeder Smith owns a great amount of property, both in this city, and New London. His property is all highly improved and therefore very valuable. His transactions for the year have been quite important.

E. C. Goff is extensively interested in pine, farming lands and city property. The past year has been quite an active one with him.

A. L. Smith does a very heavy business in the real estate line. Besides having a large amount of his own property, to care for, he is the agent for the G. B. & M. C. Co., which owns extensive tracts of excellent land throughout the northern part of this state. His sales for the past year aggregate to a large amount.

Louis Schintz deals largely in real estate and besides loans money for divers parties at home and abroad.

Geo. C. Jones has extensive investments in farming, pine and mineral lands in various localities throughout this and other states and does quite a large business every year.

J. W. Hammond handles considerable city and farm property, here and elsewhere, and does a considerable business, buying and selling, in the course of the year.

Edward West has larger real estate interests in Appleton than any other citizen and is always busy in making sales or improvements.

INSURANCE.

This has grown to be a very important business in Appleton, as might be expected where there is so much valuable property for which the people are seeking protection. Fortunately the people are provided with some of the best and most reliable agencies to be found in the state.

A. L. Smith does a leading business in this line. He represents a splendid array of companies which have nobly withstood all the severe tests with which the past few years have been attended. The owner of a policy in any one of them may be certain to have an honest loss equitably and promptly adjusted.

Conkey & Briggs conduct the other leading insurance agency in the city. and of course do a large business. Their companies are among the financially ablest in the world and afford their patrons the most absolute protection against loss by fire. Messrs. Conkey & Briggs are careful, courteous and obliging and always aim to promote the interests of their patrons.

THE POST OFFICE.

The Appleton post-office is one of the institutions of the city of which the people have just cause to feel proud. It occupies a handsome building, on Oneida Street, in the rear of Foster's store, erected expressly therefor, in the fall of 1876. It is handsomely furnished and has all of the modern appliances of a first-class office. The postmaster is G. M. Miller and M. K. Gochnauer is his assistant. The following statement indicates the amount of business transacted at this office during the course of the year:

3155 orders Issued....... ....$ 39,652.83
2150   "   Paid.................... 39,621.02
Quarter's account current......... 7,459.95

Total........................... 86,733.80

Registered letters Delivered...... 1,173
  "   "   in Transit...... 697
  "   "   Issued.......... 584

Total........................... 2,454

EXPRESS

The express office occupies a building on Oneida Street, near Lawrence. Mr. John Lester is the efficient agent who attends to the wants of the people in that line. The business of the company at this place amounts to a large sum every year. Its receipts for 1878 aggregate to $14,000, being an increase of $2,000 over last year.

TELEGRAPH

The N. W. Telegraph office is conveniently located over Clark & Edwards store and is largely patronized by the business men of Appleton. H. A. Tice is the efficient agent and is prompt and accurate in the discharge of his duties. The receipts of the office for the past year amount to $1,650 being quite an increase over the income for '77.

THE NORTHWESTERN SURGICAL INSTITUTE

This institution was established several years ago for the treatment of all manner of deformities of the human limbs and body. Its method of treatment is thorough and scientific and in accordance with rules prescribed by the most eminent and successful surgeons of the country. The institute in Appleton has been attended with a large measure of success. We have known of numerous cases, generally considered as hopeless, that have been fully and completely restored—the persons gaining the use of the deformed parts almost perfectly. Dr. Heineman who is in charge, devotes himself earnestly to his work and the patients entrusted to his charge have the benefit of his time, skill and enthusiasm. We can heartily commend the institute to all those suffering from deformities of body or limbs.

EDUCATIONAL.

Lawrence University and the Public Schools.

LAWRENCE UNIVERSITY.

It is now about thirty years since the corner stone of this institution was first laid in the then wilderness upon the banks of the Fox River. It was a bold, almost hazardous enterprise; and yet its success, almost from the beginning, was remarkable. Within six years after its first opening and before even any railroad came within many miles of the place, the number of the students was greater than is usually found in the most popular of Eastern seminaries. Its popularity was one cause of its financial difficulties. The large patronage induced by the very moderate expense to the students, occasioned an outlay which the pecuniary resources of its friends proved insufficient to meet. Debts were incurred and the most serious embarrassments followed. The very existence of the institution was for some time imperilled.

Yet through all its trying history, few institutions can boast a nobler record of educational effectiveness. There has been a large number of students, and the scholarship produced has been of a high order and recognized as such both in the East and the West. The requirements for entering the college classes are higher than those of a large majority of Western colleges, as is also the standard of attainments for graduation. Notwithstanding the gradual and very considerable elevation of the courses of study and the increased conditions of entrance within the last few years, the number of students in the college classes, instead of diminishing, has steadily increased, and the number of graduates within the last five years has been greater than in any other consecutive five years in the history of the institution.

Says Dr. Warren, President of the Boston University: "Lawrence University has reason to be proud of the Alumni she has sent to Boston. If she can keep up the succession worthily, she will very soon acquire in these parts a most enviable reputation for man-making discipline. No college has sent us better specimens of strong, cultured, practical men."

The institution while under the patronage of a Christian denomination and aiming to be a Christian college, yet opens its doors to all comers of whatsoever creed or nationality, and especially intends to furnish the best facilities to students who without property or wealthy friends are striving to help themselves to an education. The great number of this class who have gone forth from its halls and are now filling honorable stations in society, amply justify all the efforts and sacrifices hitherto made in its behalf.

The College Courses are among the highest and best of any College in the whole West.

The Preparatory Department furnishes a very thorough training for either the Classical or Scientific Courses in College.

The Academic Department affords excellent facilities for a Higher English or first-rate Business Education.

The School of Music is of a highly superior character, and is rapidly growing in popularity.

The School of Drawing and Painting is of excellent repute.

The whole number of students connected with the institution during the last year, according to the catalogue just issued, was 236, of whom 134 were gentlemen and 102 were ladies; of these 108 were in the College Classes; 51 in the Preparatory Department; and 77 in the Academic Department and in the schools of Music and Painting.

The necessary expenses of a student in the institution are unusually moderate. For ordinary Collegiate, Preparatory and Academic studies the whole cost to a student, including board, washish, fuel and light, need not cost more than from $40 to $65 per term. Extra charges are made for the Commercial and ornamental branches.

PUBLIC SCHOOLS OF APPLETON.

Number of children in each district, age between 4 and 20 years:

1st District.............................. 410
2d District..............................1,013
3d District............................... 773
4th District.............................. 282

Total............................2,478

Of this number 1,580 attended the public schools during the year, being 63% of the number of children drawing State tax.

The amounts expended for improvements in the last year, are as follows:

1st Ward...........................$ 117
2d Ward............................. 1,197
3d Ward............................. 1,626
4th Ward............................. 426

Valuation of school houses and sites:

1st District property valued at.......$ 5.000
2d   "   "   " 21,000
3d   "   "   " 13,000
4th   "   "   " 6,000

Total valuation....................$45,000

The number of teachers employed in each district with their respective salaries are as follows:

1st District, 4 teachers; Principal has $450; each Assistant, $360.

2d District, 14 teachers; Principal has $1,400; two Assistants each. $675; each of the others, $360.

3d District, 6 teachers; Principal has $800 (?); one Assistant, $540; each of the others, $360.

4th District, 3 teachers; Principal has $630; each Assistant, $360.

Total number of teachers employed in the Public Schools, 27.

Improvements are as follows: 1st District has furnished one of its departments with new seats and bought Appleton's Encyclopedia; 2d District has bought Appleton Encyclopedia and $50 worth of biographies; 3d Ward has furnished a new department with seats; 4th Ward is building a brick school house in place of the burned frame school house.

That the public schools of this city are making true progress, intellectually and morally, is evident when considering the following facts:

1st. The hard times, since the panic of 1873, have greatly reduced the prices of commodities and of all kinds of services, unless the supply of commodities has been less or the services more efficient than heretofore, thus making the demand greater and the price higher. Nearly all the schools have reduced the teachers' salaries, thus showing that the educational advancement of these schools has not been sufficiently progressive enough to make the demand greater and the price higher. But, in Appleton, the educational progress of the public schools has been such that the teacher's salaries are not merely the same as usual; but they have in some cases been increased. In the 2d District, the Principal's salary has been increased $200 a year, and one of the Assistants $75; in the 3d District, the Principal's salary has been increased (want of time prevents the writer to inform himself sufficiently as to the exact amount, but he believes it to be $125 a year), and an assistant has been employed for $540 instead of one for $225.

2nd. The teachers, at their last examination, independently and cheerfully raised the standing of the common schools; so that, next year, a child that completes the course of study adopted for the common schools, will have a fair knowledge of U. S. History and of arithmetic in its daily commercial application; a fair foundation for physical geography, resting on a thorough knowledge of discriptive and political geography; a practical knowledge of grammar; a facility to express thoughts on paper; and it will be able to read intelligibly any ordinary reading matter, and spell 98% of the words found in a Fourth or Fifth Reader. When we reflect that this is the work of seven years' schooling (a child six years of age, completing the course at 13), it must be admitted that this is all that can be reasonably expected of any school.

3d. The improvement in morals in the public schools is very marked, and especially is this the case in the 2d school district. In the fall term of '73, there were forty-three corporal punishments inflicted in the Second District by the principal, while this term there have been only eight. It must not be forgotten that in the fall of '73, less than three hundred pupils were enrolled in the Second District, while at present, there are upwards of six hundred. The suspensions have decreased from eight to one for the same time. This unparalleled success is due to the School

Board and the interest the better class of citizens manifest in our public schools. In the employment of teachers, partiality is unknown, and ability is the only criterion upon which teachers are employed. The influence the better class of citizens exert upon the schools by sending their children there, cannot be overestimated.

4th. Though the High School has existed but two years, still its influence is very perceptible; and especially is its influence very marked in the Second District. The ratio of school attendance to the whole school population in this district is 80%, which is probably a higher ratio than any other school district can exhibit in the State; and it is far ahead of Chicago, whose per cent. of attendance in '76 was only 46%. About twenty of the scholars of the High School leave yearly to teach.

This year three of last year's graduates are employed in the city and are giving good satisfaction. Though the School has existed but two years, it has now a library worth $250; a collection of corals, sponges, &c., worth $200; apparatus for the study of natural philosophy, worth $150; and there is no doubt but that the value of the library in a short time will be $500. These facts alone are sufficient to show that there is life in the School and that good work is done therein.

Instruction in the High School may be had in Book-keeping, Natural Philosophy, Botany, U. S. History, Constitution of U. S. and Wisconsin, Physiology, Moral Philosophy, Latin, through Virgil, German, Rhetoric, in Mathematics through Trigonometry. It should be borne in mind, that the faults of this School are its thorough instruction, rigid disipline, and severe examinations. No chance for idlers and drones.

WEST'S SHIP CANAL.

A CHANNEL WHICH AFFORDS WATER-POWERS OF GREAT CAPACITY AND RELIABILITY—ADAPTED TO EVERY KIND OF MANUFACTURING—AN AVERAGE HEAD OF 12 FEET—EASY OF ACCESS AND PROVIDED WITH FACILITIES FOR TRANSPORTATION BY LAND AND WATER—IMPROVEMENTS ALL MADE—SITES EMBRACING EVERY ADVANTAGE FOR SALE OR RENT AT PRICES WHICH WILL NOT ONLY SATISFY BUT ASTONISH THE PURCHASER.

The water power at Appleton, as a whole is, of course, dwelt upon at considerable length elsewhere, and we shall not here undertake to go over the same ground. Our object, in this connection, is to point out some of the special attractions for manufacturers which have been created by the building, through the heart of Grand Chute Island, of

EDWARD WEST'S SHIP CANAL

which has been accomplished at an expense of nearly $40,000. It would be difficult to conceive of a more desirable or valuable system of powers than has been created by this splendid improvement. A score of years ago, when this island was covered by a primitive and luxuriant growth of vegetation, a man without good judgment, foresight and experience would cross and recross it many times without halting to consider the

SPLENDID POSSIBILITIES

which it contained, and without stopping to consider how practical a scheme it was to make it available for great, useful and important purposes. But Mr. West was endowed with all these attributes and his "mind's eye," pictured to himself what the future would demand and what industry could accomplish. He did not wait to be pushed to this great undertaking but anticipated the wants which would spring from the future development of Appleton. Accordingly, in 1870, he set himself about the task of constructing a channel, through Grand Chute Island, for the purpose of securing a grand system of water powers, and under his direction, one reason was sufficient to accomplish it. And, in the fall of that year, therefore, it was completed and the water was directed between its banks.

THE POWER THUS CREATED

is equal to the strength of 3,000 to 4,000 horses. All this valuabe power is free from the obstructions on the banks and treacherous margins of the streams, and the canal has only to be tapped at any desired point and at once the power is ready for use. The canal is 2,000 feet in length and the width of the island is such as to give ample building lots running back on either side, while the natural channels of the island afford sufficient escape for waste water from the wheels in the highest stages of the stream.

The canal is cut in the solid gravel bed of the island, and can never suffer from washing. It has the capacity to float the largest vessels that can ever enter through the canals of the river improvement, being 130 feet between the embankments, and 17 feet from the top of the embankment to the bottom of the canal. These embankments have an average width at the base of 45 feet and are built of stone and gravel, so that they cannot suffer from wearing, freezing or thawing. On the margin of this canal manufactories of all kinds needing ready and constant supplies of power can be built with no more work to secure it than that of cutting a short race a little beyond the rear of the building, to allow the water to discharge from the wheels into the natural channel of the stream.

It is very important to say, in this connection, that this chain of powers is combined with

NUMEROUS ADVANTAGES

which are seldom if ever found. Abuting the lots on either side, of the canal are public thoroughfares, in a thoroughly improved condition, and by means of which any point is rendered as accessible as could be desired. Then the

SHIPPING FACILITIES

which are within easy reach, are as ample, capacious and varied, as could be desired. Indeed the M L. S. & W. R. R. describes a serpentine track through the heart of the island and which can now be reached at a trifling cost and with little trouble. And when the various contemplated side tracks are completed, freights can be received and delivered by manufacturers, located on this channel at their very doors, as the demands occasion it,

But enough has scarcely been said of the

LEGITIMATE FEATURES

of these powers, as they now actually exist. Of course in their reliability, they share this advantage, in common with other powers in this city. This is explained by the uniformity of the river flowage, the variation of which, during the entire year, does not exceed 30 inches. The natural and artificial arrangement of the canal affords

AN EXCELLENT HEAD,

at any point thereon, which is not less than 10 feet at any place and is as great as 16 at other points. The average head is fully 12 feet, which is ample for all or any particular purpose.

THE NEW DAM

which has been constructed is of the greatest importance to Mr. West's system of powers. It adds materially to their permanency and reliability. Indeed so far as these features are considered there is

NO ROOM FOR IMPROVEMENT left; and indeed, in any particular, it would be difficult to suggest a beneficial change.

These powers, of course, are occupied to a considerable extent now; but with their great and well known capacity, there is still room for 70 additional establishments. The remaining powers are ·

NOW IN THE MARKET and Mr. West offers them for sale or rent at prices that will discount those exacted at any other point, East or West, North or South. They are unrivalled in desirability, and those who contemplate engaging in manufacturing industries, now or hereafter, should visit Appleton, see that they are as we have represented, and then invest. Otherwise all correspondence, on the subject addressed to   EDWARD WEST, Appleton, Wis., will receive prompt and coruteous attention.

OUTAGAMIE COUNTY.

A BRIEF CHAPTER DEVOTED TO ITS PROGRESS AND PRESENT CONDITION—CHARACTER AND FERTILITY OF ITS SOIL—ITS PRODUCTS FOR THE YEAR 1878—ALLUSION TO THE EXTENT AND VARIETY OF ITS BUSINESS INTERESTS—STATEMENT SHOWING ITS FINANCIAL CONDITION, ETC., ETC.—OUR PRESENT COUNTY GOVERNMENT.

Outagamie County is situated between Lake Winnebago and Green Bay and is divided by the Fox River which runs through the south-east corner. It is bounded on the north by Shawano County, on the south by Winnebago and Calumet, on the east by Brown, and on the west by Waupaca. It is particularly well watered, the principal streams, besides the Fox, intersecting the county being the Wolf, the Shioc, the Embarrass Rivers and Black Creek. These together with their numerous and important tributaries, afford a natural water supply which is of the greatest value.

THE SURFACE OF THE COUNTY. is a delightful interchange of rolling uplands and gently sloping vallies and presents the most desirable advantages in this respect, for agricultural pursuits. There are no bluffs worth mentioning and but few abrupt elevations.

OF THE SOIL ITSELF but little need be said. It consists of a clay deposit, made during a geological epoch, not very far distant, and is rich in all the elements that enter into the agricultural products adapted to this parallel of latitude. The proof of the fertility of the clay lands is best seen in quality and extent of its products. It is specially adapted to wheat growing and the grade of this cereal is nowhere excelled by that of similar products, in any other state in the Union. Indeed, it is well known that the reputation of Wisconsin wheat, to which Outagamie County has made essential contributions, is equal to that raised in states most celebrated for this purpose. All other kinds of agricultural products are raised here with success and in abundance. Our soil is also adapted for dairying purposes and stock growing and in this direction considerable advancement has already been made.

OUR CLIMATE, of course, resembles that which is common in this parallel of latitude, but it has some important differences, however. Our summers are delightful and the "heated season" which so distresses many localities is either very much abridged here or is entirely unknown, the temperature being generally quite uniform. Our falls are long and charming—often extending well into November. Our winters are steady but vigorous and in some respects are the most important part of the year. They are usually attended with snow falls, the importance of which, is that they facilitate the handling of large quantities of fine timber in which the county abounds. But a feature which is of the greatest consequence is that our climate contains elements highly conducive to good health. Epidemics are unknown and, as a rule, the people are healthy, hearty and vigorous.

has been most gratifying. The southern portion of our county has been settled only about 27 years, but yet there
is no farming district in the state which
is more highly improved than the two
southern tiers of towns. The land is in
a high state of cultivation and most of
the work is now performed by labor saving machinery. Fine dwellings and
splendid and capacious barns adorn
nearly every farm and other improvements also are not lacking to make farm
life desirable and the county attractive.
During the past eight years the settlement and improvement of the northern
part of the county has been very rapid.
Indeed the advancement which has already been made indicates a much longer
period of labor than has been required
to accomplish the splendid result. That
section of our county includes many
highly improved farms and the buildings
are of a character which reflect credit
upon the industry and taste of the inhabitants. However there is yet consid-
able unimproved lands in the extreme
towns which can be had at a fair figure
and which offer desirable homes for people of limited means and industrious
habits.

Ontagamie has now a population of
upwards of 28,000. Notwithstanding
the unfavorable condition of the times,
the increase has been very rapid during
the past few years. Indeed, as shown
by the census reports, the percentage of
our increase from 1870 to 1875 was
greater than that of any other county in
the state; and we have no doubt that
when the increase of the succeeding
three years is known, the result will be
equally flattering.

OUR ROADS

There is no comparitively new county
in the state which has as fine roads as
Outagamie. Our local legislators have
paid special attention to this subject and
the result is that splendidly graded and
graveled roads now ramify nearly every
important section of the county.

OUR PRODUCTS FOR THE YEAR.

While the crops in many sections of
the country have been little short of complete failures, on account of the excess-
ive heat prevailing just before harvest,
in Outagamie the yield has been quite
gratifying. The following tabular statement shows the acreage of crops, in
this county for the year of 1878—being

a considerable increase over that of the
previous year:

TOWNS.	WHEAT.	CORN.	OATS.	BARLEY.	RYE.	POTATOES.
Buchanan....	2179	92	827	72	78	80
Bovina.......	559	196	325	48	42	47
Black Creek.	2116	276	314	14	37	81
Center.......	4377	752	1304	146	55	167
Cicero.......	1018	199	195	10	46	45
Dale	3059	716	754	45	126	84
Deer Creek ..	370	100	158	15	20	38
Ellington....	4359	837	1095	138	117	95
Freedom.....	3070	652	917	118	61	252
Grand Chute	3221	542	1155	319	76	188
Greenville ..	3943	590	782	10	17	93
Hortonia....	2231	689	603	46	315	70
Kaukauna ..	1546	228	823	83	....	110
Liberty	657	243	492	40	634	45
Maple Creek	1193	298	536	158	97	49
Maine	200	84	110	42	44	23
3d W. N. Lon.	22	18	30	7	6	..
Osborn	1417	376	449	16	30	44
Seymour....	1336	302	309	....	23	69
Total	36888	7190	11176	1328	1827	1580

The average yield of wheat was, at
least 15 bushels per acre. This would
make a total of this cereal, our leading
product, 533,432. Placing the average
price at 80 cents and the value of this
year's product would aggregate to nearly
one half million of dollars. The yield
of other crops was correspondingly
large. This exhibit, considering the
general unfavorableness of the season, is
most flattering. We have a large dairy
interest in this county which also con-
tributes largely to our product. The
butter product for the year is about 420,-
000 pounds; and our cheese product is
about 30,000 pounds.

THE EDUCATIONAL FACILITIES

offered here are excellent, and deserve
more than a mere passing notice, which
is all we are able to bestow. There are
now upwards of 100 school houses in
county and they have a seating capacity
of fully 6,000. Upwards of 160 teachers are employed in the educational
work.

FINANCIAL STATUS.

This is always an important subject
for consideration and it is with particular
gratification that we introduce it here,
as we believe there is no other county
in the state, the condition of whose fi-
nances can compare with that of little
Outagamie. The credit of our excellent
financial condition, soon to appear, is of
course entirely due to the wise management of our Board of Supervisors—the
local law making and governing power.
Although politically they are for the
most part of one mind —and that, we re-

gret to add, Democratic—yet, it is with pleasure that we add, that politics enter not into their deliberations. They have no pets to reward or enemies to punish, at the public expense, but conduct all their proceedings upon a purely business basis. The result is that it is one of the best governed counties in the state. As a matter bearing with great weight upon this statement, it is with pride that we point to the fact that we not only have NO PUBLIC DEBT. but always have a handsome cash surplus on hand to meet current demands Our orders are, of course, at-par, and the credit of the county stands urivalled in all respects. To show our actual condition, we reproduce, from the proceedings of the last meeting. the statement of W. H. Lanphear, Clerk, of our assets and liabilities. for consideration here:

LIABILITIES.

Amount due city of Appleton.	$1,094.93
" " town of Bovina,	289.18
" " " Cicero,	1,198.66
" " " Deer Creek	520.00
" " " Liberty,	38,82
" outstanding court cert.,	168.66
" " County orders.	1,911.65
" . accounts audited and unpaid.	3,280.39
" accounts unreported in hands of committee,	644.36
Total	9,136.65

RESOURCES.

Am't due from town of Bl'k Creek,	$ 328.55
" " " Buchanan,	2,85
" " " Center,	50.78
" " " Dale,	25.63
" " " Freedom,	117.91
" " " Ellington,	61.09
" " " Greenville	4.07
" " " Grand Chute,	61.05
" " " Kaukauna,	135.42
" " " Maple Creek,	49.62
" " " Maine,	122.60
" " " Osborn	78
" " " Seymour,	33.82
" " Shawano Co, Court expenses,	1.401.67
" " Marathon, Co. Court expenses,	411.95
" Green Lake Co. " expenses,	209.00
" " Waupaca, " " expenses,	97.00
" " Fond du Lac " " expenses,	178,00
" " Winnebago " " expenses,	219.00
" due cash on hand as per Treas. Report,	12,332.76

$15,844.45

Balance to credit of County, $6,707.70

We conclude this portion of our remarks by giving a list of the names of our county officers and Supervisors:

Supervisors—C. E. McIntosh, Chn., R. R. Batemen, A. H. Conkey, Jas. Campion, E. C. Dunn, J. T. Dreisien, C. A. Holtz, L. Huettner, Saml. Knox,

Wm. Lamure, G. W. Law, H. McDonough, F. W. Miller, P. Mulroy, P. Newcomb, F. Nolan, F. Ott, A. H. Pape, F. Petersen, J. L. Pingel, E. Pushor, W. Souders, S. H. Swift and W. Young.

COUNTY OFFICERS.

The County officers on and after the first Monday in January will be as follows:

Probate Judge—J. E. Harriman,
District Attorney—Wm. Kennedy.
Clerk—B. C. Wolter.
Treasurer—Matthias Werner.
Register of Deeds—J. A. Bertschy.
Clerk of Court—G. T. Moeskes.
Sheriff—John Brill.
Supt. of Schools—P. Flannagan,
Surveyor—E. Spencer.

MEMBERS OF THE LEGISLATURE.

22nd Senatorial District—G. N. Richmond.

1st Assembly Dist—John Petersen.
2nd Assembly Dist.—Francis Steffen.

THE COUNTY CONTINUED.

We had collected copious data from the various thriving villages throughout Outagamie County, for the purpose of showing, in detail, the amount of business and manufacturing performed in the several localities; and, of course, we had expected to utilize the same in this issue, but the work has grown to such an extent upon our hands that we are obliged to abbreviate this department more than was our original intention. We must, therefore, content ourselves with presenting the more important facts rather than submitting the details.

SEYMOUR.

The notes before us show that there has been an unusual amount of building done this year, including churches, school houses, stores and numerous tasteful and comfortable residences. Indeed, if the prosperity of Seymour is judged by what has been accomplished in this respect, it must rank among the most active towns in Northern Wisconsin, as it really is.

There is a very large amount of manufacturing done at the village of Seymour—the business in this line amounting to an extensive aggregate. Among the leading firms are Hammel & Parkhurst who manufacture flour barrel stock; Hammel & Co., hubs and spokes; J. P. Laird & Co., furniture; John Brinkman & Co., hubs and spokes; Stewart Bro's. proprietors of grist mill. Merchandizing in Seymour has also maintained to a good deal of importance and several of the establishments do a large business. The dealers are: D Hammel & Co., merchandise; Mitchel & Anderson, general stock, L. A. LeMieux, drugs; Michelstetter & Feurig, hardware, J. Dean & Sons, hardware; Philip. Muehl, furniture; J. Brinkman & Co., merchandise; Fred Rex, groceries and fruit.

The hotels in Seymour are conducted by Mr Griffith and Otto Brehmer.

In addition to the above, there are of course numerous other enterprises common to every thriving village, including boot and shoe shops, wagon making and blacksmithing, meat markets, harness making, photographing, millinery, restuarants, etc., etc.

Drs. Strong and Kerwin are the resident physicians.

From the figures before us we find that the total business, transacted in Seymour during the year of 1878, foots up to $385,000.

BLACK CREEK.

This is a prosperous town, in the northern part of the county, situated on the G. B. & M. R. R. There has been considerable building done and improvements made during the year, but we omit the details.

Manufacturing in Black Creek is a leading business and there are several first-class firms thus engaged. We particularize to some extent, as follows: Letter & Appleton manufactue lumber and conduct a grist mill; Randall Johnson manufactures lumber.

Theodore Colburn manufacturers lumber of all kinds, shingles, heading, etc., also a new stump puller of which he is the inventor; Weinburg & LeClair manufacture tight barrel staves, and F. W. Eairfield makes broom handles.

The commercial enterprises in Black Creek are quite important. The leading dealers are as follows: H. Peters, general merchandise; Geo. Loop, groceries; H. Homrig, general stock; G. H. James, drugs, notions, etc.; Mr. Naeglestock, general merchandise.

There are also numerous persons otherwise engaged, as wagon makers, blacksmiths, harness makers, shoe makers, furniture dealers and proprietors of hotels, restaurants, etc.

The receipts of business of all kinds, in the town of Black Creek, for the year amount to $92,000.

Miller & Delana have lately erected a saw mill in the town of Cicero, adjoining, of extensive capacity.

SHIOCTON

This village is situated in the town of Bovina, on the G. B. & M. R. R. The hard times of the past few years have effected it somewhat, but still it may be said that it is holding its own, and when there is a change, it will doubtless grow quite rapidly. Shiocton is in the center of a finely lumbered country and considerable of it is utilized every year by the manufacturers in that locality. The firms thus engaged are: Willy, Greene & Bertschy, all kinds of lumber; Wolcott & Balliet, lumber; Fred Spœhr, proprietor of flouring mill.

The other busidess enterprises at Shoicton are: L. Fisher, general merchandise; A. Irwin, general stock; G. P. Dickinson, drugs; W. W. Noyes & Co., groceries; J. F. Franklin, groceries; also blacksmith and wagon shops, liveries hotels, etc., etc.,

W. D. Jordan does an extensive business in the real estate line; and Parks & Hunter and a member of the firm of W. W. Noyes & Co., have a large number of men and teams employed in filling lumber contracts.

The total amount of business transacted in Shiocton for the year reaches $85,000 which is something of a falling off as compared to that of the previous year.

Our reporter accompanies his notes with the following comments.

"Business during the past summer has been unusually light. but for some weeks past has been reviving. The town now presents quite a lively appearance, and it is believed our darkest days are over."

HORTONVILLE.

This is one of the oldest, as it has always been one of the most thriving villages in the county. It contains some staunch and energetic firms, both in the line of manufacturing and merchandising. After thoroughly looking over the ground, in the labor of collecting materials for our Annual Review, our reporter submits the following truthful observations:

"During the past year our village and town have been making a steady march in the line of improvement. Industry and economy have been our guiding principle. The success that has attended our efforts in this direction has been all that we could anticipate, with existing depression in all branches in business the world over. Our business firms have wisely kept aloof from vague and uncertain speculative schemes and as a result have made a healthful growth and stand, to-day, on a firmer basis than one year ago."

Foremost among these are: H. T. Buck & Bro., dealers in dry goods, groceries, ready-made clothing, etc.; A. Græf, proprietor of grist mill and dealer in dry goods, groceries, boots and shoes; W. K. Rideout, one of the best business men in the county, manufacturer of sash, doors and blinds; J. Neusbaum, dealer in groceries, hardware, and drugs; C. A. Nye, manufacturer of pumps; Emil Schwebs and John Klein, wagon and carriage makers and blacksmiths; John Masenberg, wheat buyer. But the list is not complete until we include hotels, boot and shoe shops, tin shops, furniture stores, millinery shops, harness shops, etc., etc.

The business in Hortonville for the year amounts to $125,000.

We should say, in conclusion, that there has been an unusual amount of building done in Hortonville during the past year. The new buildings include numerous fine residences, barns, etc. Prominent among the other improvements is the building of two bridges and the reconstruction of the dam, at that place. Altogether we think that the people of Hortonville have every reason to be satisfied with the year's progress.

STEPHENSVILLE.

Our reports from this village of the business transacted during the past year show a considerable increase over the total receipts of the previous year. The list of firms, engaged in merchandising and manufacturing, is as follows: E. M. Gowell, general stock; J. S. Wunderlich, manufacturer of lumber, spokes, seeder and cultivator stock; John Regal, boots and shoes; Wm. Voss, grocery and saloon; Geo. Wunderlich, brewer; Lempkee & Wunderlich, manufacturers of brick; Henry Leveson, wagon maker and blacksmith; Wm. G. Steele, blacksmith; Star & O'Brien, blacksmiths and wagon makers; N. Mollet, wagon maker; Mr. Hoffman, furniture; W. J. Wunderlich, undertaker and dealer in furniture; M. Mollet, tailor; Wm. McGee, hotel; E. N. Pellet contemplates establishing a cheese factory.

Total business of the town for the year, $35,000.

DALE.

Some of the best and most enterprising men of the county are engaged in this town. We enumerate as follows: W. H. H. Wroe, general merchandise; V. C. Leppla, wagon maker and blacksmith; Wm. Weekel, proprietor of saw and grist mill; J. Klein, proprietor of tannery; A. Alton, harness maker and manufacturer of gloves, mittens, etc.; Jas. K. Smolk, plain and fancy painter; A. & E. Rhoades, proprietor of hotel; W. H. Spengler, general merchandise; Heuttl Bros., wagon makers and blacksmiths; P. Halpin, wagon maker and blacksmith; P. Toby, farm machinery and repairing; W. A. Balliet, manufacturer of lumber; P. Hurth, hotel and saloon.

Messrs. Young & Worden are the proprietors of the Dale fisheries. They have and are now doing a large amount of work in the line of raising speckled trout. Their enterprise is of so much importance that it is deserving of more space than we can devote to it here. We shall make it the subject of a special article, ere long.

There has been considerable building done and improvements made in the town of Dale during the past year and the people generally are happy and prosperous.

The total business of the town for the year foots up to, $77,900.

KAUKAUNA.

This is not only one of the most highly favored points in the county, but there are few, if any, in the whole country which surpasses it, having, as stated elsewhere, one of the best and largest water powers in the world. It has, as yet, been utilized only to a limited extent but its rapid development will doubtless be one of the results of the near future. Mr. John Stoveken, located there, is one of the most extensive manufacturers in the Fox River Valley. He manufactures paper on a large scale and during the past year he erected a first-class flouring mill which has lately been placed in operation.

The firm of Reuter Bros. manufacture hubs and spokes on a large scale and are doing a prosperous business.

G. W. Spaulding & Co. of this city operate a branch stave factory at Kaukauna and do a large business.

www.ingramcontent.com/pod-product-compliance
Lightning Source LLC
Chambersburg PA
CBHW021416090426
42742CB00009B/1156